BMW
3-Series (E36)
HOW TO BUILD AND MODIFY
1992–1999

Jeffrey Zurschmeide and Eddie Nakato

D1605110

CarTech®

CarTech®

CarTech®, Inc.
838 Lake Street South
Forest Lake, MN 55025
Phone: 651-277-1200 or 800-551-4754
Fax: 651-277-1203

www.cartechbooks.com

Edit by Paul Johnson
Layout by Monica Seiberlich

ISBN 978-1-61325-217-8
Item No. SA341

Library of Congress Cataloging-in-Publication Data Available

Written, edited, and designed in the U.S.A.
Printed in China
10 9 8 7 6 5 4 3 2 1x

Front Cover:
This BMW M3 is the top-of-the-line E36, and it can be pushed to extremes. The BMW 3-Series is an ideally balanced sports executive compact car that has won over millions of driving enthusiasts. Whether you have an M3 or another E36 model, this well-equipped and fine-performing car can be greatly enhanced.

Title Page:
S50 and S52 engines have BMW M POWER on the valvecovers. S52 engines carry intake-side VANOS; S50 engines do not.

Back Cover Photos

Top:
Installing the S54 engine is the easiest part of the operation. The oil pan and other parts are similar enough so that it drops right in. The challenges come with the various sensors and other connections that differ from the E36 line.

Middle Left:
Camshaft profiles have a lot to do with how the engine performs, but it turns out that changing cams doesn't have a big effect on usable performance.

Middle Right:
I installed this massive Wilwood big brake kit on the project 328i. With this much brake, I'll never worry about brake fade on the track.

Bottom:
Here's a great example of a cold-air box; air is ducted into this box from outside the car. It has no chance to heat up next to the engine before it is used. This means the air is denser and helps make more power. This can be a real improvement.

OVERSEAS DISTRIBUTION BY:

PGUK
63 Hatton Garden
London EC1N 8LE, England
Phone: 020 7061 1980 • Fax: 020 7242 3725
www.pguk.co.uk

Renniks Publications Ltd.
3/37-39 Green Street
Banksmeadow, NSW 2109, Australia
Phone: 2 9695 7055 • Fax: 2 9695 7355
www.renniks.com

CONTENTS

ACKNOWLEDGMENTS

This book would not be possible without the advice and assistance of many people, starting with the crew at AR Auto Service in Lake Oswego, Oregon. Ian Clinkinbeard did the lion's share of the wrenching on the project 328i, and its success is primarily due to his expertise. Nick Bender and Martin Sarukhanyan also took part in the project with characteristic good humor.

Steve Heino of Modern Classics did the chassis dyno work, and provided much-needed advice, and Dragan Agatonovic offered fantastic information about the turbo build process on his car. Valerie Bradley also helped me out with information about her M3 track build. Greg Meythaler of the BMW Club was also a great help. Finally, Andy Banta was a great resource of information on BMW racing and track preparation and spare parts.

I also need to thank Shari Arfons at McCullough Public Relations, Matt McCarron and Jay Baier at Turner Motorsports, Roland Graef at H&R Springs, Rajaie Qubain at Beisan Systems, Nick Fousekis at Falken Tire, Stephen Montano at Auto Tech Interiors, Joel Butzlaff at Red Ranger, and Michael Scully at Wilwood Engineering.

INTRODUCTION

BMW advertises itself as "the ultimate driving machine," which is all well and good for a TV commercial, but the fact is that no car from a dealership showroom is particularly ultimate. All production cars, by necessity, are built on compromise. If an automaker built an all-out performance car for the street, most people would hate it. It would be rough, noisy, and probably uncomfortable. So every automaker strikes a balance between performance and livability. BMW excels at this compromise, but there is still a lot of performance to be found and easily achieved in any model.

BMW started producing performance-oriented cars in the 1960s with models such as the 2002, followed in the 1970s by the first of the 3-series, the 320 and 320i on the E21 chassis. But it was in the 1980s with the E30 chassis that BMW really took off in the United States. The performance potential of the E30 was impressive by the standards of the day, and the number of BMW enthusiasts grew rapidly. But it was the E36 platform of 1992–1999 that really made the brand in America. For every year the E36 was sold, it made *Car and Driver* magazine's "10Best" list of top cars available in the United States.

The E36 3-series chassis was followed by the similarly successful E46 from 1999 to 2006. But flash forward to today and you can find that most of the E30 BMWs are now in the hands of aficionados and racers. E46 models are still in daily service, although some of them are migrating toward track use. The E36-based cars are now affordable enough that just about anyone can find a good example and build it up for street or track performance use. Parts are still readily available and the aftermarket for this model is mature. Right now is the golden era for finding and customizing the E36 BMW.

ABOUT THIS BOOK

I believe a variety of opinions and experiences make a better guide. In the course of my work on this book I've talked with folks who know E36s down to the last nut and bolt. This book is the result of extensive consultation with a great many of these subject matter experts. The experts I interviewed are quoted in this book, and the project would have been impossible without them. Most of them sell, install, and maintain the products they talk about, and their contact information is collected in an appendix at the back of the book.

This book is designed to give you necessary information as you consider various performance modifications and products available for your car. I have included step-by-step projects for common performance enhancements that can be performed in a standard garage, but this is not a comprehensive repair or maintenance manual. If that's what you need, I recommend you get an official E36 factory shop manual for your car. In fact, I recommend that you get one of those no matter what. Also, most aftermarket parts come with installation instructions, and you should always follow those instructions.

This book contains snapshot overviews of a couple of successful custom high-performance E36 BMWs, built for different purposes. These profiles show how all aspects of the car come together to enhance performance for a particular purpose, and to provide a model for you to

When completely modified, you can coax more than 500 hp out of the E36 platform, but you will want to upgrade suspension, brakes, and driveline to handle that amount of power.

Most E36 buyers simply want more performance out of their street car without making a major investment. This is easy to achieve with a few well-chosen modifications around the car.

This E36 was a 1996 328i sedan. The car came with 112,000 miles showing, and one owner for most of its life. The most important thing is that the car was completely stock and had never been seriously damaged.

consider as you plan and build your own ride.

This book would not have been possible without the cheerful assistance of many people, including Andy Banta, Ian Clinkinbeard, Nick Bender, Martin Sarukhanyan, Dragan Agatonovic, Valerie Bradley, and Greg Meythaler. Additionally, I would like to thank Ajae Wallace and Laura McShane for their patience with me as I worked on this and many other projects.

Introducing the Project Car

Example cars shown throughout this book illustrate the range of possibilities for performance enhancement, but most of the step-by-step procedures for performance modification and parts installation were performed on just one car, a 1996 328i sedan purchased for the purpose of this project.

This car had 112,000 miles and

18 years on the clock when I found it. Most of those miles and years had come under the care of the original owner. When I found the car, it was absolutely stock in every way, even though many components, such as engine gaskets, shock absorbers, and suspension bushings, were in dire need of replacement. However, everything was in working order. The initial purchase price was $3,000.

In the course of the project, we've enhanced the performance of this car by about 30 hp, and I have improved handling, braking, and interior utility as well. The step-by-step procedures in this book detail the process in every area of the car.

How to Use a Dynamometer and Read a Dyno Chart

If you have a turbocharged or supercharged car, an experienced tuning technician can assist you in fine-tuning the engine programming by using a dynamometer (also known as a dyno) to provide real-time power readings as the technician adjusts the timing and fuel map.

If you have a naturally aspirated car, including all stock E36 BMWs, dyno tuning is substantially less rewarding in power gains, but still

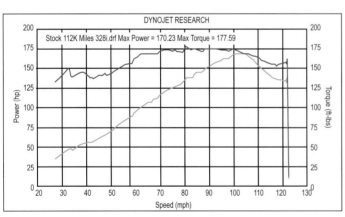

The first dyno run with the stock engine expressed over-wheel speed with the car in fourth gear. The max horsepower and torque are listed at the top of the chart. You can see that the torque curve is reasonably flat and the best horsepower is right around 100 mph.

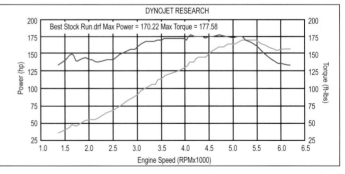

This is the same dyno run expressed over-engine speed, again in fourth gear. Engine torque is increased by 3,500 rpm and falls off after 5,000. Horsepower rises evenly to about 5,250 rpm before falling off sharply.

useful in determining how much torque and horsepower are making it to the rear wheels. Some dynos incorporate instant exhaust temperature and composition analysis, so you can be sure the combustion is optimal.

Some bench dynamometers measure the engine's power before it's installed in the car, but much more common are chassis dynamometers where you park your car on a set of big rollers and drive. Chassis dynamometers bolt directly to the wheel hubs.

Just for fun, you can also download the Dynolicious software application that works with your smart phone. This software uses the phone's internal accelerometer to calculate approximate horsepower and torque. It's cheap, reasonably accurate for the price, and fun to use!

All kinds of dynos operate by measuring the engine's ability to overcome resistance and do work, and it's important to remember that every dyno's readout is adjustable. Given the same car and the same conditions, any particular dyno may read relatively higher or lower than another. This doesn't matter. What matters is the relative improvement you get on a given dyno when tuning your car. People love to brag on their dyno sheets, and tuning shops obviously want their customers to walk away happy and advance their reputation for getting more power than their competitors out of the same car.

In the course of developing this book, I took the project 328i to a chassis dyno for a baseline reading while it was still completely factory stock. That particular dyno told me that the sturdy little E36 delivered 170 hp and 177 ft-lbs of torque at the rear wheels. At the end of the project, with new intake and cat-back

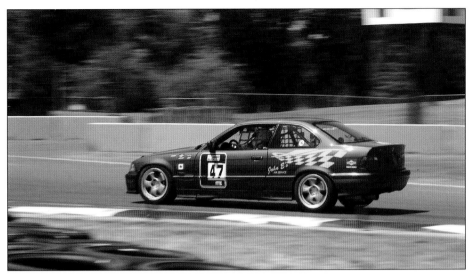

The BMW E36 is certainly a capable street car, and it does not take a lot of work to turn into a competitive track-day car. Upgrading to a combination of shocks, struts, brakes, and tires transforms even the base BMW E36 into a capable track car. If you're looking to compete in autocross, road racing, time attack, or another form of competition, the E36 is an excellent choice.

exhaust, an M50 intake manifold, and M3 cams from an S52 engine, the same dyno registered 200 hp and 175 ft-lbs of torque. The best torque was achieved at 184 ft-lbs with just a cold-air intake and cat-back exhaust. The best horsepower rating of 200, on the other hand, came at high revs with the intake, exhaust, M50 manifold, and S52 cams.

Yet when you see any dyno sheet, it's important to remember to not pay too much attention to the peak horsepower and torque, but rather, look at the entire area below the lines. The more total area you have underneath the lines, the better the power throughout the engine's operating range. After all, how often and for how long do you run your BMW at 6,000 rpm? Most driving takes place from 2,000 to 5,000 rpm. What do you have in that range, and did the work and investment in parts improve the area under the lines in that range? That's the question at the heart of real-world performance.

Building Your Car Right

Throughout the history of the automobile, we've learned a few things about going fast, staying in control, and the need to stop. We've also learned a few things about the dangers of modifying or altering the design or components. After all, the manufacturer decided it was good after spending millions of dollars on engineering and testing. Stepping out of the safety zone and modifying your car means taking responsibility for the changes you make and the effect those changes have on performance, safety, and longevity.

There's an old saying in racing, "Speed, low cost, and longevity: pick any two." I've never seen that saying disproved, but an E36 comes pretty close to picking up all three. Still, stories of blown motors, broken transmissions, and cooked brakes are all around us, and you have to understand that possibility before you start. When you exceed the power and the stress tolerance that the engineers designed into the car, you're going to break things from time to time. Only a chump tries to blame the original manufacturer when his or her customized car breaks.

You can take some tried-and-true steps to have fun and achieve a good outcome when modifying your car. Read the following and give them careful consideration before you start.

One: Play Safe

Safety must always be a primary concern when you're working on your car. I knew a guy who died when his car fell on him. He owned a set of jack stands but didn't use them that day, probably because it was just a quick little job. Get yourself a set of good jack stands and a quality large-size floor jack and use them every time.

Similarly, be smart when you're making changes to your car. Don't go out and drive hard on brand new parts or brand new work. Have other people check the work whenever possible. Even professionals make mistakes from time to time; people leave nuts untightened, forget to adjust new parts, and leave fluids unfilled. Any of these mistakes may happen to you, and if you play with cars long enough something will happen to you, probably multiple times. At best these mistakes are embarrassing, usually they are expensive, and at worst they can be dangerous or lethal. Be smart, play safe, and you'll have a good time.

Two: Learn about Your Car

You need to read and learn before you whip out a wrench or whip out your checkbook. The world is full of people who have spent a lot of money on their cars only to find that

they have a ride that is slower and uglier than when they started. The final tragedy is that they've cut up so much of the original car that they can't ever get it back to stock.

It pays to do your homework. Learn what's available for your car and what fits on your particular model. Also, learn from what others have done before you. You can purchase a full shop manual for your year and model from Bentley for under $100. Your local BMW specialty shop has valuable information and expertise for you. Enthusiast and club publications, such as *Roundel* and *Bimmer,* can keep you up to date on new products and developments. You can also use Internet forums, but bear in mind that the quality of information from these sources is highly variable.

Three: Understand What You're Doing and Why

Before you spend a penny or grab a wrench, sit down and think through what you want your car to do for you. If you're looking at competition, make sure you have the current rulebook in front of you. The worst thing you can do is show up to race with some minor modification that just landed you into the "unlimited" class in an otherwise stock vehicle.

Do you want to design your E36 for supreme handling for autocross competition? Do you want to enter hill climbs or drive at open track days at a road racing circuit? Maybe you just want to look great, sound great, and hit Cars & Coffee this summer; there's no shame in that. The point is, when you know what you really want to do, you can start your plan to get there.

Whatever your goals are, your car should be built so that it func-

tions smoothly and comfortably, in harmony with you as the driver. If you overdo one aspect of a car and neglect another, you'll have problems. Ask anyone who ever built a really fast car and never thought about his brakes! As you consider, plan, and build your car, think about balance and the real-world driving you're going to do. For example, if you go to one or two track days every year, but you have to drive your car to work every day, a set of track-ready coil-over shocks is probably not the best choice for you.

One of the most common mistakes people make when building a performance car is they try to make a car that's excellent for two (or more) very different purposes. Trust me, a performance rally car isn't going to be any good at an autocross, and a really pumped racing car makes a terrible daily driver. If you try to split the difference between two radical applications, you end up with a car that isn't particularly good at anything. Get your vision and your budget together and build your car to do one thing really well, or build it to everything pretty well.

When you know what you want to do and you understand the rules, you can usually come up with a comprehensive shopping list. That's where this book is designed to help you, by going over many common modifications people make and the major options on the market. You can read what's involved in a given modification before you decide to dive in yourself, take it to a pro, or leave that part on the shelf.

Four: Define Goals and Objectives

You need to be realistic about what you can afford and what you plan to do with your car. Diving in and modifying your car always costs more than you expect. You need to double your estimate because it'll still cost more than you expect. So make an accurate budget and realize that Rome wasn't built in a day, and neither will your car be done next weekend, or next month. That's why you see so many people driving around with half-finished cars.

My suggestion is that you start with a notebook. I use a paper notebook for each project car I have. The notebook stays in the car and I use it to log changes I make and results that I notice. Some people prefer a spreadsheet or a blog; use whatever works for you. The point is to get into the habit of logging what you've done and the results you saw. The more objective data you have (lap times, dyno sheets, and so on) the better your log is.

For most people, the car they're modifying is also the car they drive to work every day. There's usually not a lot of downtime available in the car's schedule. And some people aren't handy with a wrench, so take this to heart: if you've never done serious work on your car before, upgrading the brakes or installing a turbo on your daily workmobile is a bad way to start.

Divide your shopping list into functional areas: engine, transmission, suspension, brakes, interior, and so on. This book is divided into chapters on that basis to help you. In each functional area, list the things you want to do and the price of each item you need. Don't forget labor costs, gaskets, and fluids. If you're doing the work yourself, be sure to account for the cost of tools you need to buy.

With a good shopping list in your hands, and a total budget that

will probably surprise you, it's time to prioritize.

Most new builders start with cosmetics. This is only natural, but I think it's backward for a performance car. In general I like to improve handling and braking before I put money into the engine, and I leave cosmetics for last. Who wants to scratch or dent an expensive paint job when a wrench slips?

With your itemized and prioritized list of modifications, you should be able to make a budget and a schedule for work that fits your finances and your calendar. Don't sweat it too much if you get behind on the schedule; everyone does. Right now the trick is to enjoy the journey as much as the destination.

Five: Have Fun and Don't Overextend Yourself

One key to a successful performance build is to make sure you reward yourself from time to time. There's nothing as satisfying in a project as being able to tell the difference when you've made a change. So schedule your mods to make sure that you get a noticeable goodie from time to time. Maybe that means putting in the racing seat before the urethane bushings, but that's okay if it keeps your interest in the project.

There's a trap out there that you have to keep in mind, because it can grab you and cause no end of pain. The trap springs when you become financially overextended in your car and then run into trouble. The world is full of cars for sale where the owner has $25,000 in receipts and is looking for $10,000 or best offer by next weekend because he has to pay the mortgage. Don't be

that unhappy person if you can help it. It's worse if your car is half-done, because if you can sell it at all, it's probably worth less than when you started.

The truth about building custom cars is that you're not going to make a profit building and then selling your car. You're not even going to recoup your cash expenditures, so don't view this hobby as an investment. There's no reason to think that the person who buys your car will even think any of your mods are worth keeping. For your own protection, you should view this process as building yourself a unique car that you customized for your own tastes and no one else's.

Finding a group of like-minded people in your area can help you keep your project going. The Internet is a nice tool for learning and discussion, but folks on the other side of the country can't help you change the brakes, or give you a ride to pick up your car from the mechanic. A local club is also a good way to gain access to specialty tools. If one member has an engine hoist, then everyone has an engine hoist, and you can spend your budget on a tool that no one else has yet. Treat your club right, and you'll always have help when you need it.

The last thing to say about having fun and sticking with the project is that you should make sure that the car stays drivable, registered, and insured as much of the time as possible. Nothing kills your enthusiasm for a project car as fast as spending money that just disappears under a tarp in the garage. Keep yourself behind the wheel to keep the rewards of your project coming back to you, and that will keep your enthusiasm going strong.

E36 MODEL AND ENGINE GUIDE

Although BMW tagged the E36 with a variety of model codes, only a few variations are meaningful on the E36. In the United States, the E36 chassis was offered from model years 1992 through 1999. In that time, there were 4-cylinder models and 6-cylinder models. The 6-cylinder models were by far the most popular.

When it comes to the engines used in these cars, there are substantial differences between the 4- and 6-cylinder models and between engines of different model years. Yet these all fall into a few broad categories for North American cars. Internationally, BMW sold many more sizes and variations of models and engines than were imported to the United States and Canada, and those models are not covered.

In BMW history, 1996 was a watershed year for the E36 family. In this model year, every car in the lineup changed its engine, and many model designations changed as well. This was due, in part, to the change to federally mandated On-Board Diagnostic II (OBD-II) engine management technology.

The main difference between model designations is that the popular 325i was enlarged from a 2.5-liter to a 2.8-liter engine to become the 328i. The 2.5-liter engine was retained, however, as the 323i. This engine is identical to the previous 325i but detuned to 168 hp. This was presumably done to give the 328i a horsepower advantage.

E36 Model Guide

The following sections offer some information on the various models of E36 available in the North American market.

4-Cylinder Cars

Four-cylinder E36 BMWs included the 318i and 318ti sold in the United States and Canada 1992–1998, and the 320i sold in Canada 1993–1995.

It is worth noting that the 318ti hatchback and the Z3 roadster and coupe are substantially different

The M52 engine simply carries "BMW" on the valvecover. You can also tell this engine from an M50 by the bulge for the VANOS system on the intake side.

Maintenance and Repair Schedule: The 80,000-Mile Rule

As the E36 series has aged, mechanics have had the opportunity to notice trends in required repairs. What they have found is that 80,000 to 100,000 miles or about 8 to 10 years of service is a watershed for these cars. A number of items consistently need attention at that interval. Almost all E36 cars are well past that mileage at this date and are now coming up on their second rounds at 160,000 to 180,000 miles, or 16 to 20 years of service.

If you have not yet purchased your E36, keep these items in mind as you compare candidate cars. Ask to see service records for claimed maintenance and repairs. If you already own your E36, consider the accumulated mileage on your car and look over this list for items that you have not yet checked or repaired.

- The cooling system is mainly made of plastic, and the entire system needs to be replaced about every 80,000 miles. Wear symptoms include cracking in the radiator neck, tanks, hoses, thermostat housing, and water pump.
- Engine pulleys, the idler and tensioner especially, must be replaced about every 100,000 miles. While you have that all apart, the oil filter stand O-ring gasket generally needs to be replaced at the same time.
- The stock flywheel is a dual-mass assembly designed for smooth takeoff and shifting. This wears out at roughly 100,000 miles and must be replaced. For performance builds, a solid single-mass flywheel is a good upgrade. Single-mass flywheels are also less expensive than the OEM dual-mass replacement.
- The driveshaft flex disc (also known as the Guibo) and driveshaft center support bearing must be replaced at about 100,000 miles.
- Manual transmission shift bushings must be replaced at about 100,000 miles. This is a good opportunity to upgrade to a short shifter.
- Engine and transmission mounts may be oil-soaked and decayed. Check and replace these as necessary at 80,000 miles.
- The valvecovers for 1996 and later cars are plastic that hardens over time and has a tendency to crack. This creates a vacuum leak that throws off engine tuning and may trigger a check engine light. Valvecover gaskets also harden and require replacement at about 80,000 miles.
- If the cooling system has failed at 80,000 to 100,000 miles and the engine has overheated, check the cylinder head for cracks and leakage. The stock E36 water temperature gauge does not read hot until the engine is very hot and damage to the head is likely to have occurred. Plus, E36 cylinder heads are known for cracking with age, even if overheating has not occurred. ■

The water pump is just one of many components on the E36 series that must be replaced every 80,000 to 100,000 miles. If you're shopping for an E36, pay careful attention to the mileage and ask for maintenance records to show that required tasks have been completed.

Looking at the E36 engine bay, you see a lot of plastic. Many of these components become brittle and crack over time and mileage. Specifically, the radiator and cooling system components are a frequent failure point at about 80,000 to 100,000 miles.

from all other E36-class vehicles in that the chassis and rear suspension are not the same. The rear suspension on these cars is a carry-over from the older E30 BMW line. Therefore, procedures in this book relating to the rear suspension and chassis are not directly applicable to these cars. The front suspension and steering gear are common to all E36 cars.

The 318i sedan, however, is a true E36 chassis and step-by-step projects relating to the rear suspension and chassis are applicable to these cars, if you can find one in the United States.

The M42/M44 series 4-cylinder engines are a carryover from the E30 line but are equipped with DOHC and four valves per cylinder, with an iron block and aluminum heads. These engines feature strong forged cranks and header-style exhaust manifolds in the long block and a Bosch Motronic ignition that eliminated the distributor in favor of individual coils.

Weak points in these engines included coolant gaskets in the timing case, which allowed coolant into the oil sump. The M44 engine series adopted in 1996 eliminated this problem, and the updated parts can be installed on the M42 engines.

318i (1992–1998)

The 318i sedan, 318is coupe, and 318ti hatchback used the M42B18 engine from 1992 to 1995. This engine displaces 1,796 cc and generates a maximum of 138 hp at 6,000 rpm, and 129 ft-lbs of torque at 4,500 rpm.

For the 1996–1998 model years, the 318 series switched to the slightly larger M44B19 at 1,895 cc, developing the same 138 hp at 6,000 rpm and improving slightly to 133 ft-lbs of torque at 4,300 rpm.

320i (1993–1995)

Canadian buyers were offered the E36 with the traditional M50B20 engine displacing 1,991 cc in the 320i. This engine was good for 148 hp at 6,000 rpm and 140 ft-lbs of torque at 4,300 rpm. This model was not offered in the United States, but some examples may be found.

6-Cylinder Cars

By far the greatest number of E36 chassis sold in North America included some version of BMW's inline 6-cylinder engine. This started with the 2,494 cc M50B25 in the 325i line in 1992. The M50 engine family used a cast-iron block and aluminum alloy head, with four valves per cylinder and DOHC. After the 1992 model year, E36 models in America received the M50B25TU engine, which featured variable cam timing on the intake cam only. BMW called this VANOS, an abbreviation of its German name.

The M50 line was upgraded to the M52 line for the 1996 model year along with the advent of OBD-II across the North American BMW line. European versions of the M52 used an engine block made from Nikasil aluminum; North American engines used an iron block due to high sulfur concentrations in American fuel. In 1999, the M52 received a technical update to implement VANOS on the exhaust cam as well as the intake, but the M52TUB28 engine was never sold on the E36 chassis. However, this engine can be retrofitted for a small boost in mid-range torque.

The most powerful of the 6-cylinder engines were the S50 and S52 series, used in the U.S.–market M3 editions of the E36. These engines used the same heads and engine block as their more prosaic counterparts but were enlarged in both bore and stroke and included high-performance cams and valvetrains to increase performance by about 50 hp.

325i (1992–1995)

The 325i was introduced in 1992 as a four-door sedan or two-door coupe using the M50B25 engine, displacing 2,494 cc and generating 189 hp at 5,900 rpm. Maximum torque was 181 ft-lbs at 4,700 rpm. The engine featured a bore of 84 mm and a stroke of 75 mm.

The 325 series was updated to the M50TUB25 engine for 1993, featuring the same 2,494 cc displacement

The 325i series was available with two or four doors, with the two-door bearing the designation 325is. This series carried the M50 engine of 2.5-liter displacement.

but with slightly higher compression and VANOS variable intake cam timing. Horsepower and max torque remained the same, but max torque now came at 4,200 rpm. This engine was in use until the end of the 325 line in North America at the close of the 1995 model year.

328i (1996–1999)

For the 1996 transition to OBD-II in America, BMW selected the M52B28 engine with 2,793 cc of displacement and changed the 325i into the 328i.

Like its predecessor, the M52B28 engine offered four valves per cylinder and DOHC with VANOS. To create the extra displacement, the new engine used the same 84-mm bore as the M50B25 engine, but extended the stroke to 84 mm as well, creating a "square" engine geometry. The 2.8-liter engine produced 190 hp at 5,300 rpm and 210 ft-lbs of torque at 3,950 rpm. This engine was used throughout the E36 328i production run, ending in 1999.

Interestingly, the 2.8-liter engine did not produce any more horsepower than the 2.5-liter, but the increased stroke added 29 ft-lbs of torque, making the 328 a much better performer at lower RPM and the best low-cost candidate for performance upgrades.

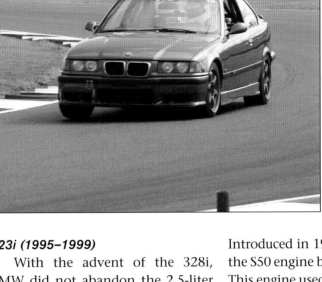

The M3 was BMW's factory hot rod E36. First released in 1995, the S50 engine produced 2,990 cc of displacement, 240 hp, and 225 ft-lbs of torque. The S52 was released starting in 1996 at 3,152 cc and the same horsepower, but with 240 ft-lbs of torque.

323i (1995–1999)

With the advent of the 328i, BMW did not abandon the 2.5-liter engine but instead updated it to M52 standards, creating the M52B25. This engine was used in the new 323i 1996–1999, violating the convention of putting the displacement in the last two digits of the model code. The 323i engine still displaced 2,494 cc with a bore of 84 mm and stroke of 75 mm, but it was detuned to 168 hp, presumably to provide more of a performance difference with the 328i. Torque remained the same at 181 ft-lbs at 3,950 rpm.

M3 (1995–1999)

For serious performance enthusiasts, the best E36 variant is the M3.

The 328i used the longer stroke of the M52 engine to produce almost 30 more ft-lbs of torque than the 325i. The M52 also supported OBD-II engine management; the previous M50 engine did not.

Introduced in 1995, the first M3 used the S50 engine based on the M50 line. This engine used the same fundamental cast-iron block and aluminum cylinder head as the M50, but with lighter pistons, upgraded connecting rods, better cams, stiffer valvesprings, an improved exhaust manifold, and an optimized cat-back exhaust system. The new engine featured a square bore and stroke at 86 mm, yielding 2,990 cc of displacement and 240 hp at 6,000 rpm and 225 ft-lbs of torque at 4,250 rpm. The S50 engine can be identified by the "BMW M Power" logo on the plastic engine cover.

But like the rest of the E36 line, major changes were in store for the 1996 model year. The S50 was upgraded to the S52, which remained in place until the end of the E36 line in America in 1999. The S52 is based on the M52 line in the 323i and 328i models. The S52 engine offered an increased displacement of 3,152 cc courtesy of an 86.4-mm bore and 89.6-mm stroke. The combination produced the same 240 hp at 6,000 rpm, but boosted torque to 240 ft-lbs at 3,800 rpm.

The M3 also included upgrades in suspension, brakes, steering, and

S50 and S52 engines read "BMW M POWER" on the valvecovers. S52 engines carry intake-side VANOS where S50 engines do not.

bodywork, making it the top choice for stock performance. However, M3 models cost more to purchase at all levels of age and condition, and performance enhancements from the already high level of the M3 come at an incrementally greater cost.

It is worth noting that apart from the valve size and displacement, the M52B28 and M52B25 engines use the same head and block as the S52. M3 cams are a direct replacement on these engines, so some smart work on the valvetrain can bring a lower-cost 328i much closer to M3 engine performance.

Project: Swapping an E46 S54 M3 Engine into an E36 chassis

If you are looking for a lot more power in your E36 chassis, it is possible to swap in an S54B32 engine used 2001–2006 in the E46 series M3 and the 2001–2002 Z3 M and the 2002–2008 Z4 M. Before you set out to achieve this, however, be aware that this is a very difficult and expensive project.

You can tell the difference between an S52 and S54 visually because the S54 engine simply has an "M" logo on a plastic engine cover, whereas the S52 has a plastic cam cover that reads "BMW M POWER."

Internally, the S54B32 used a larger 87-mm bore that results in 3,246 cc of displacement compared to the S52 series at 3,152 cc and the 1995 S50 at 2,990 cc. Both the S50 and S52 delivered 240 hp in U.S. trim, and 225 or 240 ft-lbs of torque respectively; the S54 boosts output to 333 hp and 262 ft-lbs of torque.

The S54 engine makes its power with the displacement increase and by using a new cam design with high-pressure infinitely variable double VANOS on both the intake and exhaust sides, plus increased com-

pression to 11.5:1 (from 11.3 in the S52). With the E46 engine, you also get the European-style individual throttle bodies for each cylinder. The engine also offers other incremental efficiencies.

The good news is that the S54 drops right in to the E36 chassis, and it saves you from extensive modifications required for other engine

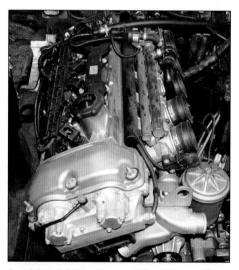

Looking at the front of the S54 engine, you can see the double VANOS bulge on both the intake and exhaust sides of the cam cover.

The S52 in this 1997 M3 was upgraded to the later S54 found in the E46 M3 series. This new engine makes 333 hp and 262 ft-lbs of torque.

Unlike the E36 series engines, the S54 engine offers an individual throttle body for each cylinder. All of the E36 engines used in North American production offer a single throttle body leading to the intake plenum.

swaps. No modifications are required to the firewall, crossmember, or any other fixed parts of the chassis. You do need the BMW/Siemens MSS54 engine management control system, more commonly called an electronic control unit (ECU), but BMW official nomenclature is DME for "digital motor electronics." The S54 does not run at all with an S52 or any other stock BMW DME. The engine mounts and pickup points are the same. The oil pan has a different shape in some areas, but these do not impact the crossmember or other features in the engine bay.

The project is made more difficult and expensive by the extensive modification and adaptation necessary to fit all the ancillary components and connect the older systems to the newer engine. Because the S54 engine uses an entirely different DME, that unit requires its own wiring harness and then an adapter harness as well to connect the chassis, engine, and DME.

The mechanics of this engine swap are comparatively simple, but the list of required additional parts is long. Here's a rough shopping list to complete the swap:

- Drive-by-wire accelerator pedal
- S54 wiring adapter harness
- S54 transplant wiring harness
- Z3M engine wiring harness
- S54 DME and EWS (German abbreviation for electronic drive-away protection) and key
- S54 exhaust adapter pipe
- S54 catless header set
- Sport clutch kit
- Full replacement of gaskets, seals, and hoses

In all, the price of the S54 engine, extra parts, and labor to do this job can be expected to total as much as $15,000 to $18,000 before the car is ready to drive.

To remove and replace the engine in an E36, follow the specific procedure in the factory shop manual, but the following are some guidelines to give you an idea of what's involved.

Follow These Steps

1 Disconnect the driveshaft. At the rear of the driveshaft, four 13-mm bolts connect the driveshaft to the final drive unit. Rotate the driveshaft and loosen each of these in turn.

At the front of the driveshaft is the Guibo flex disc. This is a doughnut-shaped part made mostly of rubber but reinforced with steel. The front of the driveshaft has three bolt holes in a flange, and the tailshaft of the transmission has three holes on a flange as well. The Guibo has six holes, and the tailshaft and driveshaft are installed so that they use alternating holes in the Guibo.

All bolts are installed with the nuts at the forward end of the car because there's no room to put the bolts in from the transmission side. Use a socket on the driveshaft side and an open-end wrench on the transmission side to undo the bolts. Once loosened, you can use a small pry bar to separate the driveshaft from the Guibo because the driveshaft is in two pieces and has a splined center fitting that slides to make room.

When you remove the Guibo, note that it has an arrow cast into the side to indicate which direction faces forward.

Tip: Use the parking brake to hold the driveshaft in place while you work. Release the parking brake to rotate the driveshaft.

At this time you must also disconnect the shift lever from the transmission, which makes this a good time to do a short shifter conversion if you have not already made that upgrade.

2 Now disconnect the transmission from the engine and remove it from the underside of the car. The transmission is connected to the engine at the bellhousing, and there is a supporting crossmember toward the rear of the car. All these must be removed with the transmission well supported on a stand or jack.

You need to remove the clutch to remove the engine. As part of the engine replacement, you should replace the stock clutch with a high-performance aftermarket model.

3 Remove the clutch assembly and flywheel to lighten the engine. The clutch is held on with bolts around the perimeter of the pressure plate; the flywheel uses a smaller circle of bolts to connect to the crankshaft.

4 Remove the catalyst section from the exhaust header. Set these aside. If you have not already upgraded the exhaust, now is a good time for that job.

Profile: Valerie's E36 M3 with an S54 Engine

Valerie Bradley went through the process of installing the S54 engine from the E46 series into her E36 M3 sedan. Here's why she went to the expense and effort, and what she got out of building this street car into her track-day machine.

"The car is a 1997 M3, and I wanted to put more power into it. The stock engine was fine but wasn't spectacular on the straights. I knew that there was more in the car than I could find with that engine. The VANOS was going bad, so instead of fixing that, we decided to put in a new engine," Valerie says.

Among the options Valerie considered was a turbocharger kit and just buying a newer car with more power. But there was a good reason to stick with the E36. "Part of the reason for getting the older car was that we're putting it on the track and that can be dangerous. I didn't want to have that much money at risk on the track. So we decided to upgrade this car until we're at the limits of what the car can do," she says.

The swap to the E46 engine was more complicated than expected, but the results have been spectacular. "With the new engine, the car was dynoed at 297 hp at the wheels. It was a significant enough power increase to be worth the effort and money. I can actually pass people on the straights now. The car is more lively, more fun, and more nimble. There's so much more it has to give now," Valerie says.

In addition to the new engine, Valerie has installed a set of Moton coil-overs for suspension, Alcon front brakes, and an aftermarket radiator that was not required in order to clear the E46 engine, but does a better job of keeping that engine cool on track. Plus, the aftermarket radiator incorporates an oil cooler, which is absolutely necessary for the high-revving S54 engine. ∎

With the S54 engine installed, Valerie is ready to drive her 1997 E36 M3 on its first track day.

The new S54 engine works great. You must use the digital motor electronics (DME) computer from the M3 model, and an adaptive wiring harness is needed to install that DME in any other E36, but all the major mechanical points bolt right up.

5 Disconnect the engine wiring harness from the chassis wiring harness. The connection is made through a barrel connector on the right-hand side of the engine. Removing the harness is simply a matter of unscrewing the barrel connecters on the driver's side near the firewall and removing the gang-plugs. Once loosened, the plugs pull right out.

These barrel connectors are the points where the chassis wiring harness meets the engine wiring harness. Disconnect these before you lift out the engine.

6 Disconnect all hoses and the grounding strap that links the engine to the chassis. Remove all ancillary components, such as the alternator, power steering, and AC pumps. You need to remove the serpentine belt first, and then simply unbolt each component from the engine. The power steering and A/C units have their own attachments to the car's chassis, so set them aside in the engine bay but leave their pressure lines connected. You just want them off the engine.

One point at which engine replacement becomes hung up, literally, is the engine ground strap. Be sure it's disconnected before you try to lift the engine out of the engine bay.

7 Remove the nuts that hold the aluminum engine mounts to the body-side mounts. Use a socket wrench on an extension to get down to the nuts, but you should not need air power. They should come loose easily. The body-side mounts are large cushioned doughnuts that can move around when loosened.

When you install the new engine, bear in mind that you can move these mounts to get a good fit before tightening them again.

BMW engine mounts are remarkably simple and straightforward. Undo the nuts and the engine lifts right off. The body-side mounts are movable so you can adjust the new engine to fit perfectly.

8 Locate the lifting tabs and connect the lifting chain to them. There is one on the front and one on the back of the engine. Use a rag to cushion the chain against any part of the engine that it touches while lifting, and then carefully lift out the engine.

The engine lift point at the forward end is located right around the VANOS hardware. A convenient lifting loop is provided for you, and this attaches to strong points on the engine for safe lifting.

With the clutch and flywheel off, the S52 engine lifts out of the engine bay quite easily. Be sure you've drained the oil before you begin, as it's much harder to drain with the engine out.

The flywheel is already removed from this engine for the lifting process, but you can also see the rear lifting tab, which you find on the driver's side just behind the cylinder head.

9 Installing the new S54 engine is a reversal of the removal process. Using the same lift points, and with the flywheel and clutch removed for extra clearance, gently and slowly guide the engine into place. You need to locate engine mount arms from the 2001–2002 S54-equipped Z3 to fit into the E36 Chassis. Make sure the engine mounts are loose enough to move around a little bit to fit everything together.

Here's the body-side engine mount, with its rubber isolator and vibration dampener. This mount moves around a bit so you can position the engine onto it and then tighten everything into place.

The engine mount is fixed to the side of the engine and made of cast aluminum. This is a great place to grab on and move the engine around, but make sure your hands are out before settling the mount onto its pad.

Installing the S54 engine is the easiest part of the operation. The oil pan and other parts are similar enough that it drops right in. The challenges come with the various sensors and other connections that differ from the E36 line.

10 After the engine is installed, the real work begins. First, the project requires a custom radiator, and the DME from the E46 M3 is absolutely required to operate the dual VANOS system. You can purchase the radiator through any of the main aftermarket BMW houses such as Turner or Bimmerworld, and all of these are direct replacements. No modifications of the radiator core support are required.

This custom radiator incorporates shrouding, an electric fan, and a separate aluminum overflow tank. This does a much better job for a performance build in the long run.

The stock radiator is a good unit, but those plastic tanks are prone to cracking. If you're investing the money in an S54 engine, buy an aluminum high-performance radiator. They don't cost much.

You can see how all the fittings are TIG welded on the custom radiator. If you want a new water temperature gauge or electric fan thermostat, this is the way to do it.

11 Then, the wiring harness connections for emissions controls and engine performance sensors have to be adapted to the E36 chassis. This is where you use the adapter harness I mentioned earlier.

Once all of the connections are made to the S54 sensors, the DME calibrates itself to stock parameters, but most builders choose to take the car to a tuner at this point for custom programming.

UPGRADING EXHAUST COMPONENTS

The fuel charge in an engine does its work by expanding as it burns, pushing a piston down in the cylinder. Once the fuel charge has accomplished this task, an efficient engine evacuates spent exhaust gases as quickly as possible, although turbocharged cars scavenge a bit more energy out of the gas on the way out. The exhaust system performs this very simple function, and the exhaust is a great place for you to easily bolt on some low-cost horsepower and torque.

Tip: A note of common sense: Always replace all gaskets and worn fasteners when replacing exhaust components. Exhaust leaks are easy to avoid and a pain to fix.

But before you work on the exhaust, bear in mind that the exhaust system is also a critical emissions control system. Both federal and state laws govern what you can and cannot do to your car.

About Catalytic Converters

The catalytic converter has been the cornerstone of automotive emission controls for the past 35 years. Controlling emissions from street cars is an important environmental concern. Cars today are far cleaner than in decades past, thanks in large part to improvements in catalyst technology.

The catalytic converter is a muffler-type device that uses a ceramic or stainless steel alloy web that holds reactive catalyzing material (usually palladium or rhodium). When the exhaust gases pass through the catalytic converter and heat the catalyst, a chemical reaction occurs

The exhaust system does much more than just produce a sexy sound. This is a critical performance item in the build, and you should consider your purchases carefully, and in concert with the other engine modifications.

A replacement high-flow catalyst can really help improve airflow through the system, which means more power under your right foot. If you drive on the public roads, be sure to stay on the right side of the law by running a catalyst. Modern ones have no performance drawback.

that helps change carbon monoxide to carbon dioxide, and helps to burn off any unburned hydrocarbons that remain in the exhaust stream before it exits your car.

For a modern car designed to work with at least one catalytic converter, the presence of a catalyst does not mean you can't increase horsepower. The entire engine management system is designed to work with the catalyst and provide good performance. If you are concerned about the catalyst being restrictive, or you think it might be plugged-up, you can buy a new high-flow replacement unit.

Prices for new direct-fit catalytic converters for E36 models range from $500 to more than $1,000, depending on your model, so this is not a decision to be made lightly. Aftermarket "universal" catalysts cost much less and may be welded into place, but results vary widely. At a minimum, make sure that the inlet and outlet diameters for any aftermarket catalyst match those on your car. And bear in mind that with older cars such as the E36, some changes may have already been made to the factory parts. Check your car's actual system. Also, check to be sure that any aftermarket catalyst fits in the available space and does not knock against the car's floorpan. In general, you are better off spending the money on a direct-fit catalyst designed for your E36.

Although extreme high-performance applications generally include removing one or more catalysts from the exhaust system, it is a violation of U.S. federal law to do so on a car registered for use on public roads. Moreover, removing the catalysts makes it harder, if not impossible, for your car to pass emissions testing, and removing the catalyst on any OBD-II car (1996 and newer) will likely cause a check engine light.

Be aware that an illuminated check engine light is an automatic emissions testing failure on all OBD-II cars. Simply clearing the light and driving to testing while the light is still off does not bypass this requirement, as the OBD-II system

Legal Aspects of Catalytic Converters

The laws that govern catalytic converters are strict. It is illegal to remove a functional catalytic converter even to replace it with a newer or better one. It is also illegal to tamper with emission control devices. The anti-tampering law applies to individuals as well as to businesses. Individuals may be fined as much as $2,500 for each vehicle tampered with, and businesses are subject to fines of up to $25,000.

Generally, you are allowed to install an aftermarket converter for these three reasons only:

1. If the converter is missing from the vehicle when the car is brought in for exhaust system repair.
2. If an inspection has determined that the existing converter has been lead-poisoned, damaged, or otherwise needs replacement.
3. If the vehicle is more than 5 years old or has more than 50,000 miles (8 years/80,000 miles for 1995 and newer vehicles) and a legitimate need for replacement has been established and appropriately documented (such as a plugged converter or unrepairable exhaust leaks).

Manufacturers of new aftermarket converters are required to offer a 5-year/50,000-mile warranty on the converter shell and end pipes. New catalysts must also be guaranteed to meet the Environmental Protection Agency

(EPA) emission performance standards for 25,000 miles when the vehicle is properly used and maintained.

The EPA requires that a new, legal replacement catalytic converter must be properly labeled. Required labels on the converters have a series of letters and numbers in the following format:

N/XX/YYYY/ZZZZ

Here's what that label means:

N = a new converter
XX = manufacturer's code issued by EPA
YYYY = a numerical designation of the vehicle application or part number
ZZZZ = numeric month and year of manufacture

Converters manufactured for sale in California may have the letters "CA" in the first position. Because California standards are more stringent than federal EPA standards, these converters meet EPA requirements and are usually known as "50-state" units. Catalysts that comply with federal laws but not California regulations are known as "49-State" units. If the new catalytic converter does not have this kind of label it may not be a legal replacement part for any U.S. application, placing you in violation of federal law.

reports that the car has not driven enough miles to report reliably on engine condition. Testers see this and fail the car for emissions testing wherever such tests are required.

Cat-Back Exhaust Systems

As the name implies, a cat-back system replaces the factory exhaust from the last catalytic converter to the exhaust tips at the rear of the car. This section of the exhaust system is where the mufflers are found. Desirable features in this part of the power system are high exhaust gas velocity and free flow with as few bends as possible.

Most aftermarket exhausts keep the basic tube size close to stock for the model of car to maintain exhaust gas velocity. Because of chassis size and underbody differences, exhausts that fit the 325/328/M3 models do not generally fit the 318 or 323 models. However, cat-backs fit two-door or four-door E36 models alike.

When choosing an aftermarket exhaust, apart from tubing size you need to look for smooth bends and joints in the pipe and unrestricted mufflers. Generally speaking, the freer the flow, the louder the exhaust, so there's a tradeoff you need to understand before you buy. If you plan to drive your car daily, excess noise can become annoying and may be illegal. If you are building a dedicated track car, noise is usually less of an issue (within the bounds of the track's noise limits).

Horsepower and Torque Gains from Cat-Back Systems

Exhaust manufacturers often claim gains of 5 to 15 hp and a similar torque improvement from a good cat-back exhaust. The actual gain depends on several factors beyond the product you choose:

- What model of E36 are you upgrading? An M3 probably sees more benefit than a 325i or 328i because of the increased amount of air already flowing through the system.
- Have you already upgraded the cold-air intake, intake manifold, exhaust header, and catalytic converter mid-pipe?

- Engine tuning is necessary to fully realize the benefits of a less-restrictive exhaust.

In general, you see the best results if the exhaust is the most restrictive part of the system before the upgrade, but most people perform the easy cat-back exhaust upgrade before they do the more difficult and expensive header and catalyst upgrades. The catalyst is usually the restriction point, and as noted above, for legal reasons a catalyst delete pipe may not be an option.

The market offers many quality cat-back exhausts, and the main thing you care about is the way they sound. Some products have a drone at certain RPM levels, and some are quieter than others. Much of that difference depends on what's been done to the engine already, because all aftermarket systems were designed and tested using otherwise stock cars. As with other parts, you're going to get what you pay for, so beware of false economy. Akrapovic, Dinan, Magnaflow, Corsa, and Supersprint are generally well known for excellent results and they fit like original equipment. Off-brands tend to have fitment issues and use thinner metal and lower quality mufflers.

All aftermarket exhausts fall into the same general envelope of performance enhancement; there's only so much power you can get out of a cat-back. If you go with a well-known and respected brand, you have a good unit that installs easily with the stock hangers. Custom exhaust systems with weld-in mufflers, such as Flowmaster, generally require more work to install, and you won't really get any additional power benefits.

The Corsa (RSC Reflective Sound Cancellation) cat-back exhaust for the BMW 328i is a quality piece of equipment. The stainless steel construction, TIG welding, great exhaust note, and performance enhancement all make this modification worth doing.

Project: Upgrading a Cat-Back Exhaust

The heart of the Corsa exhaust is the RSC mufflers, and the great-looking exhaust tips. The reflective sound cancellation system is designed to prevent exhaust drone by shaping the interior of the muffler to reflect and cancel sound that would otherwise build into a standing wave. One other reason to spend the money on a reputable, quality cat-back is the fit: A cheap unit may not have the proper clearances and can melt the bumper cover.

This project installs the Corsa RSC (Reflective Sound Cancellation) cat-back exhaust system on the project 1996 328i. This product uses twin 2.25-inch OD T-304 stainless tubes and dual mufflers. Inside the mufflers, the exhaust gases pass straight through; the mufflers are designed to reduce noise without impeding gas flow. With the previously installed cold-air intake, this is an obvious next step in performance modification.

Tip: If you're considering installing a limited-slip differential or reinforcing the rear subframe mounts, now is a great time to do that, as you have to remove the exhaust from the car to do those projects.

If you have access to a safe automotive lift, this project is easy and convenient. You can do the work using only jack stands, but it takes longer and is more difficult. Always follow the manufacturer's specific instructions.

Follow These Steps

1 Disconnect the battery and raise the car. There's no risk of electric shock, but this resets the DME so it recalibrates to the new exhaust. To ensure that the DME is completely drained and reset, disconnect both battery leads and remove the battery from the car. Then zip-tie the positive and negative battery leads together with the clamps touching for about 30 minutes to completely drain the DME capacitor while you are working.

2 Unbolt the stock cat-back exhaust segment from the rear end of the catalytic converter. Remove the four bolts that connect the two pipes. These are 13-mm bolts and nuts, so you need two wrenches. One pipe connection is a slip-fit and the other uses a ring gasket, but be sure to catch and save that gasket as the pieces come apart! Next, unbolt the exhaust hangers on either side of the mufflers, while supporting the rear end of the exhaust. With the hangers loose, the exhaust should come loose and drop out easily.

Tip: Spray some WD-40 lubricant on the rubber exhaust hangers and work them off gently because the rubber hangers are easy to break.

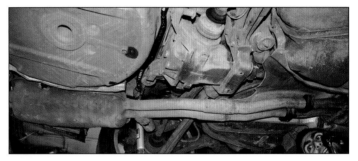

To begin the installation, place the car in the air. You can see the old, stock cat-back on the bottom.

3 Exhaust systems tend to rust far more than other areas because their heat cycles encourage the metal to soak up moisture from the air, and because of water splashed up from underneath the car. Plan on some work to lossen these nuts and have some penetrating oil and a heat source, such as a handheld propane torch, ready to go.

Apply the oil and wait, then apply heat from the torch to the nut. Patience helps loosen a lot of rusty parts, but if you have to cut the system apart, an angle grinder is the easiest and least expensive method. Just plug in the angle grinder and turn it on. Then hold the grinding surface to the stuck nuts and grind them until the part comes free.

With the exhaust bolts disconnected (or broken, or cut through) you can start to separate the cat-back section from the rest of the exhaust.

4 Remove the exhaust hangers from the stock exhaust unit and place them on the aftermarket replacement. The stock hangers can be reused on the outboard sides of the mufflers if they are in good condition. New OEM replacements should be used if the old hangers are suspect or broken. The hangers are not symmetrical and the larger space should be oriented toward the exhaust tips.

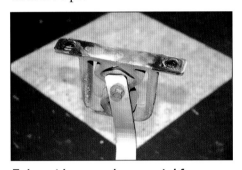

Exhaust hangers have metal frames supporting rubber mounts, to help let the exhaust move in relation to the other components, but to keep it within boundaries.

Use the shop stand (or make one) to support the front end of the cat-back exhaust while you're undoing the hangers at the rear of the car.

Simply install the existing hangers back onto the Corsa cat-back exhaust. If the rubber is decayed or broken, replace the hanger.

5 Position the new exhaust to the car and adjust the fitment of all parts. Make sure you put the ring gasket back into its space between the catalyst section and the cat-back section. Then, working front to back, tighten the bolts throughout the system. Make sure the exhaust is centered in its space at the bumper and that adequate clearance is provided all around. Run your hands along the top of the exhaust path and anywhere that the heat shielding is too close to let your fingers by, press it up and out of the way.

One side of the exhaust slides into the new cat-back, while the other side simply mates with a ring seal. This is to allow for easy installation.

Installing the ring seal into the exhaust is important to prevent stinky and annoying exhaust leaks. It's a tricky fit-up process sometimes so take your time.

Tighten the side with the ring seal first. The slide-in section of the other side holds itself in place while you work.

6 Reconnect the battery and lower the car to the ground. You are ready to test-fire the car. Listen for rattles and exhaust leaks, which often make a ticking sound. Your car should sound absolutely fantastic, with a throaty purr that changes to a roar when you go to wide-open throttle.

Tip: With all stainless steel exhausts, any residual oils and fingerprints "burn" into the surface of the exhaust the first time you start the engine and heat the unit. It is important to properly clean all polished areas or areas that you want to maintain cosmetically with brake cleaner or a similar product before you start the car for the first time after installation.

The exhaust tips come out right where they're supposed to be, the mark of a well-made cat-back exhaust.

7 You may have a vacuum-actuated exhaust valve on your E36, and this valve is not present on an aftermarket unit. Simply fold this tube back on itself and zip-tie it closed, then tuck it up out of the way.

Whenever you work with stainless steel, wipe all oils and fingerprints off the metal before you fire the engine. The oils in your fingerprints burn into the steel and leave permanent marks.

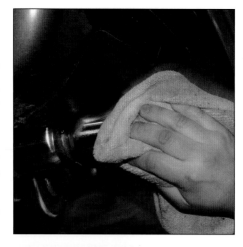

Here's the vacuum hose that operates the exhaust control valve. You can fold it back on itself and seal it with a zip-tie.

You can see how well the Corsa system fits under the final drive and suspension components. It sounds great and should last the life of the car.

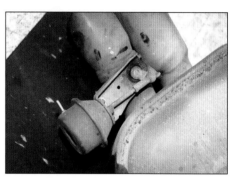

One thing you give up on the cat-back system is the exhaust control valve. But this does nothing for performance, and really doesn't need to be there.

Project Results

All of the claims of big horsepower and torque gains are just marketing until you put the parts on your car and then put your car on the dyno. I installed the Corsa RSC cat-back system and took the project 328i back to the same dyno where I made the baseline tests and ran new dyno pulls under the same conditions to see how much power the cat-back really made.

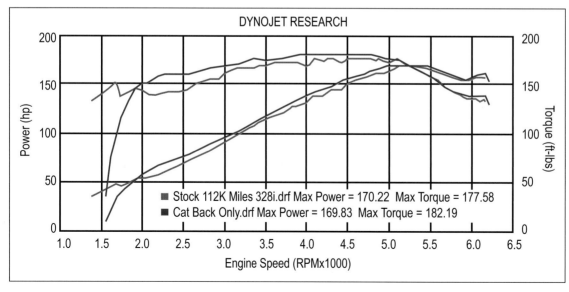

This dyno run shows the stock horsepower and torque lines in blue compared to the power made with the Corsa RSC cat-back exhaust in red. You can see that the Corsa makes more power and smoother power at all levels up to 5,000 rpm, and then matches the stock system above that.

This dyno comparison is expressed relative to engine speed (RPM). The test showed that on this day, I actually lost a tiny amount of maximum horsepower compared to the test with the stock system shown in the introduction of this book. The stock setup showed maximum horsepower of 170.23, and this fell to 169.82.

We did see a maximum torque gain of almost 5 ft-lbs from 177.59 to 182.19, and the arc of torque is wonderfully flat. In addition to the gain of maximum torque, the value is more than 160 ft-lbs by 2,200 rpm and rises steadily to the maximum at about 4,400 rpm, then stays over 160 until about 5,400 rpm.

Peak horsepower and torque are not the most important goals for increasing street car performance. Rather, you should focus on increasing horsepower and particularly torque through the rev range or the total area underneath the lines. With the cat-back exhaust in place, both horsepower and torque come up quicker and smoother than with the stock system. This means more actual power that you can perceive from the driver's seat throughout the car's operating range.

Also, notice in the dyno chart that with the stock setup, the torque and horsepower lines are quite choppy, indicating that the stock system is not well-tuned. When I installed the Corsa exhaust with reflective sound cancellation, both the horsepower and torque lines smoothed out a great deal owing to the tuned nature of the exhaust system.

The most important thing revealed during the test was that the cat-back section of the exhaust was not the most restrictive part of the system. We would have seen bigger horsepower and torque gains if the exhaust had been the part holding the car back. The dubious distinction of the most restrictive component almost certainly goes to the mid-pipe that includes the stock 18-year-old catalytic converters or to the M52 intake manifold, but it's also likely that the stock exhaust manifold plays a role, along with the stock air intake. I discuss modifications to those components next.

Exhaust Headers

The exhaust headers attach directly to the body of the engine at the exhaust ports on the cylinder heads. On all E36 engines, the exhaust ports face the right (passenger's) side of the car; you have two manifolds for the forward three cylinders and rearward three cylinders. For 1992–1995 325 and 1995 M3 cars, the exhaust manifolds are made of cast iron. The 1996–1998 units for the 323, 328, and M3 are made of lighter welded tubing.

The main thing you want in a header (and throughout the exhaust system) is efficient flow of gases on their way out of your car. This means a reasonably sized pipe with a few smooth bends and no restrictions. It's good for this pipe to be wrapped or coated on the outside to keep heat in the exhaust gas until it exits your car. It's also good for this pipe to be made of stainless steel, although stainless is brittle and prone to fail-ure when exposed to high heat or large amounts of vibration.

For heavy-duty applications, such as racing or extensive track day use, the more malleable mild steel is a lighter and more durable choice. For street use, cosmetic purposes, or corrosion resistance in salt-air cli-mates, stainless is a better choice. You may also choose to have the

The stock BMW exhaust header is very good by most standards, but torque and horsepower improvement can be obtained by a quality aftermarket replacement. Be sure that the product you select works with the mid-pipe and the cat-back system.

exhaust coated with ceramic, such as Jet-Hot coating, inside and out to reduce gas friction and heat loss (hotter gases are less dense and lighter), and to move gas through the system to the exit more efficiently.

Finally, if you're shopping for a header, you can find some with long primary tubes of equal length converging into two pipes. Each primary tube is generally about 1.75 inches. These headers help to tune the exhaust by making sure that each exhaust pulse comes through the system at its own time. The stock unequal-length manifolds allow pulses to come through at the same time at certain RPM.

Most BMW headers offered for the E36 are similar in length to the factory manifolds, and aftermarket headers are mid-length. It is almost impossible to fit a true long-tube header in a BMW engine bay; these are generally a custom-made part if you want them. Most of the aftermarket "long tube" headers for BMW E36 models are really mid-length headers.

Many designs are possible, but the most popular and effective header setup is to use the factory routing and factory termination point. Using this arrangement, you can fit the exhaust system with standard mid-pipes, catalysts, and so on. As a rule, cylinders 1, 2, and 3 feed one header and cylinders 4, 5, and 6 feed the other header with the exit flanges mating to the factory catalytic converter section.

When considering which headers to buy, the primary factors are the fit and finish of the item. Many of the budget aftermarket headers either do not fit, or have extremely thin walls and will melt under the higher exhaust temperatures seen in high-performance engines. Some

Header, Mid-Pipe, and Catalytic Converter Fitment

One factor to consider with exhaust headers is whether you are able to use them with the stock mid-pipe and catalytic. If the header does not fit, it can be expensive and difficult to modify it to fit with the stock mid-pipe. If you also replace the mid-pipe and catalytic converters, this can also be expensive and can be difficult. Your best option is to seek out an exhaust header that is a well-known name brand that is known to match the stock mid-pipe. These can be found new or used.

inexpensive headers have oxygen sensor bungs placed in locations where you cannot fit the oxygen sensor, and some do not quite mate properly with the mid-pipe. High-quality exhausts manufactured by companies such as Supersprint and Akrapovic are your best option for ease of installation and usable lifespan. However, you pay more for the quality you're getting. Another option is to use the European BMW headers. These are usually available on the used market, and are of extremely high quality and durability. They may not flow as much as some of their aftermarket counterparts, but they flow better than the U.S. market stock units and have OEM fit and finish, so they definitely work in the engine bay.

Finally, it's important to recognize that an exhaust system is indeed a system, and piecing together headers, pipes, and catalytic converters is never as effective as a designed system. You want to keep an appropriate amount of resistance (generally called back pressure) in the system, and make the pipes small enough to keep exhaust gases flowing at the right velocity. The exact optimum setup varies from engine type to engine type, and by the RPM range that makes the horsepower and torque. Unless you buy a complete kit (such as those offered by well-known BMW suppliers) or have a lot of time and resources to dyno-test multiple configurations, you're generally limited to the commercially available products.

For racing, the only considerations are flow and meeting the noise limits set by the racetrack, and all racetracks have them. A large muffler generally restricts exhaust sound while flowing very well.

INTAKE MODIFICATIONS AND FORCED INDUCTION

At its most basic level, an internal combustion engine is an air pump. Air is sucked into the front and pushed out the back. In this chapter, I examine how air is sucked in through the intake and air filter to the intake manifold and the combustion chambers. In the case of turbocharged and supercharged engines, I discuss how air is pulled through the turbocharger, then pushed through the intercooler into the engine.

Performance enthusiasts should never lose sight of the fact that all of the air that the engine is going to use to make horsepower has to come in through the air filter, and has to go out through the tailpipe. You need to remove horsepower-robbing restrictions from the entire path. If you were watering your lawn and realized not much water was coming out, and you looked at the length of hose and realized it was kinked in the middle, you'd unkink it and fix the problem, right? That's basically what you have to do with the engine's intake and

Here's a great example of a cold-air box; air is ducted into this box from outside the car. It has no chance to heat up next to the engine before it is used. This means the air is denser and helps make more power. This can be a real improvement.

The cold-air intake is simply better for filtering air and getting it into the engine. The stock system was designed to be inexpensive to produce, and to keep water and particles out of the engine no matter what you do to the car. The CAI is designed to be efficient. The materials don't matter to the function, but that carbon fiber sure looks great.

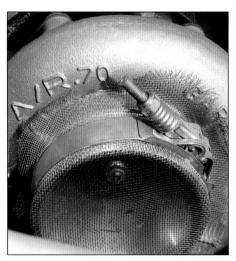

A turbocharger offers a big step up in performance, but it costs a lot of money and you're way out of the safety zone with any kind of forced induction. Plan on spending a lot of money if you go this route.

exhaust systems. You must figure out where the kink in the hose is (where the restriction is happening) and correct it. That's the key to performance.

Within reasonable limits, all products and upgrades discussed in this chapter are aftermarket solutions applicable to naturally aspirated E36 engines. No North American–market E36 models used forced induction from the factory, so any such modifications depend entirely on aftermarket parts. Those projects are generally too involved for the home mechanic to undertake, so although I discuss at them, I didn't attempt them myself.

Engine Performance

An internal combustion engine is a marvelous piece of technology. For the most part, modern engines run longer, smoother, more reliably, and produce more power per cubic centimeter of displacement than any mass-produced engines ever sold to the public before.

A bewildering array of products claim better flow, more pounds per square inch (PSI) of boost, and a cooler intake charge. Generally, more power is what you're after. But before you dive into your project engine and install a bunch of parts, you need to develop a build-up plan, because each part affects the function of other parts. The engine operates as a system and its parts are interdependent.

And because an engine is a system based on the flow of gases, the tightest point in the system generally governs the total output. The classic demonstration is to attempt to breathe through a drinking straw. It doesn't matter that there's a room full of air, or that your mouth could gulp in a lot more air; the total oxygen available in that case is what you can suck through that straw.

What this means in real terms is that you may see an incremental improvement in power by relieving a restrictive component in the system, but real power gains require thoughtful modification to the entire system for the most efficient flow and greater energy output.

The Science of Combustion

A tablespoon of gasoline and a quart of air have a finite amount of energy potential held within them. We can change that potential into different forms of energy such as heat, motion, and light by putting the fuel and air into an internal combustion engine. You can theoretically create perfectly efficient engines and drivetrains, but you can never get more energy out of that spoonful of gas and bottle of air than the native elements hold. So to make more power in your car, you have to put more of those elements through the

system, and make the system as efficient as possible.

Inefficiency can include such flaws as not burning all of the fuel you put into the combustion chamber. These are the "unburned hydrocarbons" that are measured in many emissions tests. This happens when the air/fuel mixture is incorrect. The theoretically perfect mixture is called stoichiometric and is about 14.7 parts air to 1 part gasoline. The reason you care is that if you have an imperfect mixture, you're not getting all the energy you can out of the fuel and air.

To that end, everything you change is about putting more air and fuel through the system. I discuss replacing the stock air intake and filtration with a more direct and less restrictive product, and how to make that air flow faster into the engine with the use of a more advantageous intake manifold. Finally, I look at aftermarket solutions to change the engine to forced induction, with the caveat that such modifications are typically far more expensive than simply installing a better engine or purchasing a later model 3-series that was turbocharged from the factory.

Engine Air Intake

The easiest step in improving engine performance is to look at your E36's air intake. You want the least restrictive system you can possibly find that provides clean cold air to the engine. You really do need a filter, though, because all kinds of stuff can be sucked into the engine otherwise. The front end of every car is sprayed with road debris all the time. Nothing good has ever been reported about feeding dirty water and rock chips into a BMW engine.

Here's what most stock air filters look like after a few years. That slab of paper never flowed very well, and now it's all clogged up. Time to replace the whole system.

You can gain about 4 hp and 4 ft-lbs of torque here, and maybe a little more. If you do nothing more than purchase an aftermarket high-flow air filter, you will see some benefit. But for just about $100, you can take the next step to a high-performance engine.

Another improvement that goes with an improved air filter is what racers call a cold-air box. If you remove the stock airbox, a bare aftermarket air filter pulls in air that has passed through your car's radiator or intercooler (or both) and is hang-ing around the hot engine bay. To bring in truly fresh air requires some ducting and separation of the intake point from the rest of the engine bay; do this right and it sets you apart in both performance and engine bay dress-up.

Cold-air intake kits are available from virtually every E36 aftermarket manufacturer.

Mass Airflow Sensor

All E36 models have mass airflow (MAF) sensors in their intake flow. The MAF sensor is a delicate little device that tells the DME how much air is coming in through the air filter. Positioning the sensor is crucial if you want an accurate reading; and you do want an accurate reading or the mixture will be wrong. E36 MAF sensors use a "hot wire" design that measures the amount of air passing through by the "windchill" on the filament. A secondary intake air temperature sensor corrects the MAF output for the temperature of the incoming air. Because the MAF output depends on accurate cooling of the hot wire, these devices are very susceptible to dirt and oil. It is vital that you use a high-quality air filter (and don't over-wet the oiled varieties!) to keep the MAF clean and functioning correctly.

The MAF sensor measures airflow by the cooling of the hot wire, and the DME calculates how much air it has by assuming that you're using the stock intake. If you change to an intake that is even slightly smaller or larger, the DME does not make the correct calculation because the DME works based on the stock intake pipe diameter. If you put on a larger diameter pipe, it flows more air than the DME is calibrated for, so the mixture is lean. A smaller pipe flows less air than the DME is calibrated for, and the mixture is rich. That's why aftermarket intakes tend to end right before the section of pipe that contains the MAF sensor. After the MAF sensor portion of the intake, the air passes into the intake manifold, which I discuss separately.

So, to choose a cold-air intake (CAI), you're mainly looking at where the intake gets its air and the flow capacity of the filter. Any of the available cold-air intakes on the market flow enough extra air

Here's another kind of cold-air box. This one relies on the hood being closed to seal the air intake filter off from the rest of the engine bay.

The mass airflow (MAF) sensor is one of the most important parts of the car. It measures how much air is entering the engine, and that allows the DME to decide how much fuel to offer. If the MAF becomes dirty or the size of the tube in which it sits is changed, it cannot accurately report airflow, and the DME cannot adjust the timing curve or fuel map to optimize performance.

Project: Upgrading an Air Intake

over the stock unit to give you all the benefit you need. I selected the most inexpensive CAI I could find. As with the cat-back exhaust, there's only an incremental power gain to be found here. Once you have smoothed the intake path, brought cold air to the intake, and installed a clean, new filter, the rest of the differences between individual units are comparatively small.

You can confidently select from any of the popular CAI units on the market. Brands such as Dinan, BMP Design, Injen, Active Autowerke, AFE, and Eurosport all make good products that give you about the same benefits.

For this procedure I installed Injen's cold-air intake for the E36. This kit retails online for $130 to $150 and includes an air filter, a tube that leads to the MAF sensor tube, some installation brackets, and a heat shield. The whole system installs in the same part of the engine bay where the stock airbox goes.

The stock air box and MAF. You can find a few horsepower here by changing to a nice cold-air intake setup, and give yourself a little more space in the engine bay as well.

Follow These Steps

1 Disconnect the battery. This is not to prevent shock so much as to re-initialize the DME. You should not be close to any wiring in this project.

Tip: Cover the engine with a blanket when working with the retainers and screws on the under-hood duct (or any time you're working in the engine bay). A dropped washer or screw can become wedged among all the parts on the engine and cause a world of trouble.

2 Remove the air inlet from the air filter box. This flattened tube brings air in from behind the headlights and simply disconnects from the air filter box. This part can be stored or discarded because you won't use it again.

Then remove the stock airbox. Two spring-clips hold the airbox to the MAF sensor tube. Undo a mounting bolt on the right side of the box as you're looking at it from the front of the car and the entire box comes out as one piece.

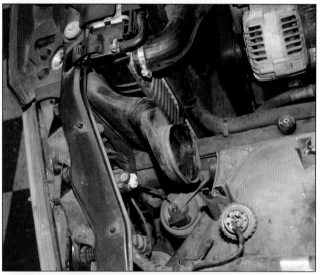

This snorkel delivers air from just under the hood to the stock air intake box. Remove it, because you have plenty of cold air through the grille.

Here are the parts to the Injen cold-air intake. I bought it on eBay. The smooth metal tube, cone filter, silicone fitting, and heat shield are all good quality parts.

30 BMW 3-SERIES (E36) 1992–1999: HOW TO BUILD AND MODIFY

3 Install the new heat shielding as instructed for the kit. The heat shield mounts to the chassis with some self-tapping screws and uses the existing support studs for the stock airbox. I drilled starter holes for the new screws to ease the installation. In the case of the Injen kit, I found that the edge of the heat shield made contact with the upper radiator hose. To eliminate the risk of abrasion, I trimmed back the heat shield to clear the radiator hose by a few millimeters.

Do not discard the heat shielding; bringing in cool air is one of the most important functions of the intake, as cool air is much denser than hot air. If anything, you may want to fabricate additional pieces

The heat shield installs to the chassis rail with these self-tapping metal screws. They have a little drill bit in the point to help them start.

to further isolate the intake from any air that has passed through the radiator or had a chance to heat in the engine bay.

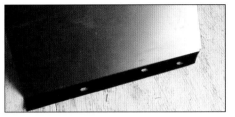

Some of these holes line up with studs that are already on the chassis rail, and some use self-tapping screws to fasten the shield.

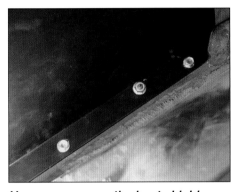

Here you can see the heat shield installed with the self-tapping screws and the stud that attached the stock airbox.

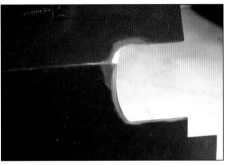

I found that the heat shield wanted to rub against the radiator hose, which could lead to a cut hose down the road. So I used the bench grinder to create a little more clearance for the hose.

The heat shield has been bent in a sheet metal brake to fit into its space perfectly.

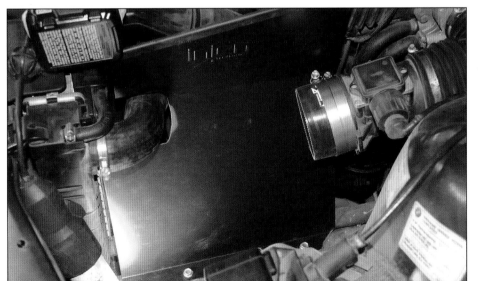

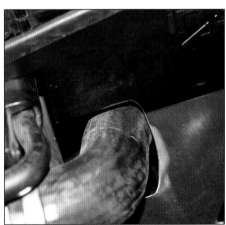

There's the hose with the modified heat shield. It could use a little more clearance toward the top.

With the clearance to the hose fixed, the heat shield is installed along with the silicone fitting to the MAF tube.

4 Place the rubber adapter around the end of the new intake tube and install the two large hose clamps loosely. Install the short ram tube by slipping it over the MAF sensor tube. Turn the new intake tube to orient the air filter end with plenty of space around it, and to match to the support bracket. This bracket mounts on the fender wall where the old airbox also mounted.

Carefully fit the new intake tube snugly against the MAF sensor tube. You know if it is not snug because it is not even all around. When oriented, install the mounting bracket and tighten its nuts and bolts, and tighten the hose clamps.

The silicone connector fitting holds the MAF tube on one side and the cold-air intake tube on the other. Hose clamps keep everything in place.

The cold-air intake tube has a bracket that helps support its weight, and it attaches to the same place the stock unit used for support.

5 Install the new air filter. Virtually all aftermarket cone filters come pre-oiled from the factory, so you don't need to add oil. But take a moment to note the maintenance schedule for the filter so you can clean and oil it (or replace it) as needed. Use the hose clamp that came with the air filter to tighten it to the intake tube.

This cone filter offers a lot of surface area, and it's out in the open so you can see when it becomes dirty. Some cone filters can be washed; read the instructions on your kit for cleaning information.

I found that one extra bolt was needed to hold up the other stock components that relied on the original air intake bracket for support. A used 10-mm bolt, nut, and washer from the metric fasteners bin did the trick.

6 Clean the engine bay of tools and any loose hardware. If you use a towel or blanket to protect the engine from loose parts, remove this as well. Reconnect the battery and turn the car's key to the "on" position for 10 seconds to re-initialize the DME. Then start the car and carefully inspect the engine bay for good connections and correct operation.

Tip: Carefully inspect your work before you test-drive the car. With all the manipulation you performed, it's easy for a connection to come loose. Any disconnected tube can cause a check engine light to come on shortly after you start the car. If this happens, check the intake air path and make sure all tubes are properly connected. If you find and refit a disconnected tube, the light may remain on for a few restarts. If the light does not go off soon, seek professional help.

The mounting bracket is not optional; without it the weight of the filter and vibration of the car would shake the filter and intake tube loose in minutes.

Our cold-air intake looks great installed and brings a bit of color to the engine bay as well. It sits right in the airflow through the grille and is protected from the worst of the engine heat by the heat shield.

Project Results

After this modification, I was back on the dyno to compare with the previous readings. This figure overlays the cat-back exhaust only with the cat-back in combination with the cold-air intake. Both the cat-back and cat-back plus CAI runs were taken within minutes of each other under the exact same conditions. The only difference between those runs was the substitution of the aftermarket CAI in place of the stock air intake.

A True Cold-Air Box Delivers Performance

Another improvement you might consider is what racers call a cold-air box. The stock system draws air from near the engine bay's right front corner, where a great deal of dust, water, and other yuck is flying around. Most aftermarket intakes pull in air that has passed through the car's radiator or intercooler (or both) and is hanging around the hot engine bay.

To bring in truly fresh air requires a completely separated part of the engine bay to pull outside air from a protected inlet. The Injen kit is a good start, but if you have the skills and tools, consider cutting some more sheet metal to isolate the air filter from the rest of the engine bay and provide it with cold airflow from a dedicated inlet. You can use simple pop-rivets to attach more pieces to the existing heat shield that came with the CAI. This is all custom work, but if done right it sets you apart in both performance and engine bay dress-up.

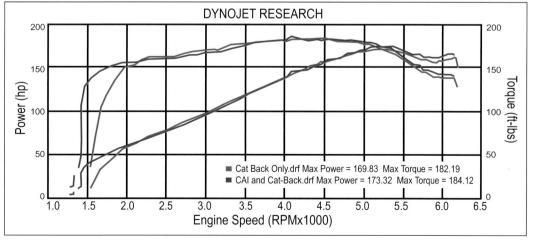

DYNOJET RESEARCH

■ Cat Back Only.drf Max Power = 169.83 Max Torque = 182.19
■ CAI and Cat-Back.drf Max Power = 173.32 Max Torque = 184.12

I gained a couple of horsepower and a couple of foot-pounds of torque with the CAI. Comparing against the stock intake with the cat-back system, all gains came above 5,000 rpm. This tells us that the intake was not the big restriction point in the system.

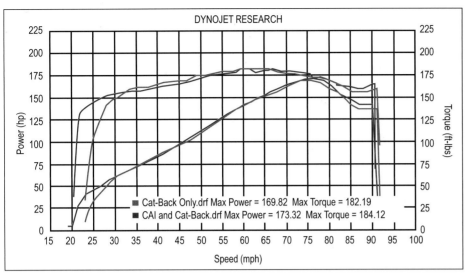

Looking at the same data expressed against wheel speed shows us that the cold-air intake really starts working for us at about 70 mph in fourth gear.

While the car is on the dyno, you can see a real-time readout of exhaust gas mixtures and the basic air-fuel ratio. This lets you know if the car is running lean or rich at any point.

Looking at the dyno chart comparing the two setups by engine speed (RPM), you can see that the cold-air intake produced 3.5 more maximum horsepower and boosted maximum torque by almost 2 ft-lbs in addition to the improvement from the cat-back alone. The best readings came at 4,100 rpm for torque and at 5,300 rpm for horsepower.

Considering the dyno chart expressed in relation to wheel speed, you see that the best torque is happening at about 60 mph in fifth gear, and best horsepower at just under 80 mph.

This tells you that the stock intake was restricting the engine's airflow a little bit, and you improved that. But as before, the maximum is not the whole story. You can see that both horsepower and torque are much improved at low RPM. Both figures rise faster and stay a little higher at the top end. So you actually put a good amount of power under the lines at the low end of the engine's range and continue right up to redline.

From the driver's seat the difference is more dramatic than it appears

on these charts. The engine is more eager to rev and the difference in perceived engine power is satisfying.

Later in this chapter, I install the M50 intake manifold, and in Chapter 4, I try out M3 cams. After each modification I dyno the car again on the same dyno under the same conditions to achieve accurate estimations of the benefits of each project.

E36 Intake Manifold

The intake manifold is designed to bring metered air to the engine. This is a simple function, but the design of the intake manifold is crucial to performance. Each cylinder in the engine has its own intake tube coming from the intake plenum to the port on the cylinder head. The length, diameter, and shape of that tube have a profound effect on how much air can flow into the engine and how fast that air is moving at a given RPM. Because power comes from moving air and fuel through the engine, those val-

ues dramatically affect the engine's power output.

In a naturally aspirated engine, a longer intake manifold tube induces more velocity for the air entering the engine, so the air is rushing in faster. This is good for horsepower at lower

Here is the next project to increase horsepower and torque. The intake manifold from the earlier M50 engines offers larger runners that are capable of flowing more air.

RPM, because the engine depends on moving as much air as possible into the cylinders in a very short cycle. A longer intake tube delivers more low-end torque because it increases the velocity of the air coming into the engine. Thus, more air can be

Look at this intake manifold for the M52 engine. The runners are small and widely spaced to help air velocity at the low end of the RPM range, but that's not where you want to make power.

You can readily see the differences between the two manifolds. On top you see the intake manifold runner from the M52 manifold. On the bottom the M50 manifold runner is much larger and capable of flowing more air at all RPM.

drawn in during the time the valve is open. At higher RPM you want to maximize the air volume, so shorter and wider intake runners are the desired combination.

This distinction is far less important when using forced induction, but it's an important consideration for naturally aspirated engines. The more engine displacement you have, the more intake velocity and volume you need at low RPM. You can only have one intake manifold design, so there is a tradeoff between low-end torque and high-end horsepower.

You can apply these principles in your E36 by installing the early 1992–1995 M50/S50 engine intake manifold on the later M52 or S52 engines. This manifold was delivered with the 325i, and it is quite different from the later 1996–1998 intake manifolds delivered with the 328i. The early M50 manifold is also often described as an OBD-I or Pre-OBD-II manifold versus an OBD-II manifold.

The earlier M50 manifolds had larger runners, and the size of the runners is perfectly matched to the ports on the cylinder head of the M50, S50, M52, or S52 engine. However, the later M52 intake manifold uses smaller runners, so there is a difference in the tube size when the manifold meets the cylinder head.

When an M50 manifold is installed on an M52 engine, the change delivers 10 to 20 extra horse power at the high end of the rev range. But keep in mind, a corresponding torque loss may occur at the low end of the rev range.

Whether this is an acceptable tradeoff is a decision for you to make. The M52 engine generally produces excellent torque, so many drivers have elected to make this modification. If you plan to change to a shorter final drive ratio, as I did with the project 328i for this book, and you have also changed to a less restrictive cold-air intake and cat-back exhaust, you may find that you have adequate

low-end torque and you can afford to trade a bit off for high-end power. In this case, the M50 intake swap may provide much-needed high-end horsepower with very little practical downside.

You can generally source a good condition M50 manifold for $100 or less online or through local salvage yards. Obviously, online sources may cost a little more, but you won't have to go dig it out of a junkyard car, either. As with all used parts, beware of buying broken or junk parts that cannot be repaired.

Tip: E36 engines are extremely sensitive to vacuum leaks in the induction system and emissions controls. Engine gaskets such as fuel injector O-rings, intake manifold gaskets, and the valvecover gasket are made of rubber or plastic and are therefore subject to hardening and cracking over time. Always replace all gaskets and O-rings when upgrading the engine to avoid vacuum leaks.

Project: Installing an M50 Intake

Installing the M50/S50 intake manifold on an M52 or S52 engine is a straightforward process. You need an adapter kit for the later OBD-II vacuum connections and a gasket set, but this modification is generally achievable by yourself in your garage. Be sure to check all mating surfaces to make sure they are absolutely clean, as any vacuum leaks in the system allow unmetered air into the engine and could cause severe damage.

The challenge with this installation is that the evaporative emissions system, including the crankcase ventilation valve, idle control valve, and other connections used to control the M52 engine are not compatible with the earlier manifold and must be adapted to the earlier part in order to complete the project successfully.

You must use some kind of adapter to complete this project. All these connections must be maintained at the intake manifold to avoid a check engine light and emissions trouble.

Some enthusiasts have worked around this problem with silicone tubing setups, and several manufacturers provide adapter kits at various price points. I chose the Turner Motorsport kit because of its excellent fit and finish and the full set of required gaskets, fittings, and custom parts that come with the kit. The Turner kit is more expensive than some other options, but worth the price in my opinion for its completeness, quality, and ease of installation. If you did not purchase a kit with a full set of plugs, caps, gaskets, and so on, be sure to read through the project to create a list of required parts for the kit you purchased.

You need sockets, extensions, male Torx tools, a knife or razor, and a heat gun or flame source to activate heat-shrink tubing to complete this project. If you are using the Turner kit, detailed instructions come with the kit. Having a shop manual on hand is also a good idea.

To mate the M50 intake manifold to the M52 engine, you need an adapter. The M52 has more connections to the manifold and this Turner Motorsports adapter makes the process easy.

Follow These Steps

1 Use a fuse-pulling tool to remove the fuel pump fuse (find the listing of fuses in the owner's manual or on the lid of the fuse box) and start the car. Let the engine die as its fuel supply runs out. Also open the fuel filler cap. This relieves all pressure in the fuel system.

Opening the fuel filler also helps eliminate fuel pressure problems when working on the system.

Pull the fuse to the fuel pump and run the engine until it dies to eliminate fuel pressure in the system before you start working.

2 Disconnect the battery. You want the DME to be reset when you start the engine again at the end of the procedure, and you will be working with induction system electronic connections at the injectors. Follow the procedure for draining the DME capacitor later in this chapter.

3 Clear the area around the manifold completely. This includes removing the fuel rail cap, the housing around the cabin air intake by the firewall, and the entire induction path from the air filter through the MAF and including the throttle body attached to the manifold. Coolant lines and an electronic throttle position sensor attach to the throttle body. The coolant lines use standard hose clamps and easily pull free. Use a no. 2 flathead screwdriver to turn the little heads on the hose clamps counterclockwise to loosen the clamps. Then remove and plug the coolant hoses to keep the throttle body away from the manifold area.

The crankcase breather tube has simple twist-disconnect attachments at both ends. Disconnect the breather tube and pull the alternator cooling hose free. It pops right off. Disconnect the center barrel connector between the brake fluid reservoir and the fuse box. The top of the barrel connector simply unthreads with a counterclockwise turn.

Detach the MAF and remove it along with the cold-air intake. You use the same MAF and throttle body with the new manifold.

You can see the MAF connector that offers several data pins to provide airflow information to the DME.

This corrugated tube is the stock solution for getting air to the throttle body. I don't have a better solution.

Here is the throttle body for the M52. North American S52 engines use the same kind of arrangement. All the air for the engine passes through this butterfly plate.

You can see the O-ring on the mating face of the throttle body here. This seals against the manifold opening to make sure that the only air getting into the engine is air that has passed through the MAF.

4 Disconnect the two barrel connections for the oxygen sensors under the fuel rail cap, and take a photo or tag the connectors to be sure that they return to their proper places on reassembly.

Unplug the connectors for the oxygen sensors. You have to undo these to do this project.

You also need to undo and remove this tray that's part of the cabin-air intake system. You can't access the rear end of the intake manifold with it in place.

5 Disconnect the crankcase vent valve, the idle control valve, the three rubber hoses for the air pump solenoid, the fuel pressure regulator, and the purge valve from the underside of the manifold. Loosen any hose clamps that keep these tight, but once loosened they pull right off. Take a photo to be sure that everything goes back on the way it was. You can leave the temperature sensor.

Next, disconnect the oil dipstick bracket from the manifold, and disconnect the manifold support brackets from the manifold and the engine. The support brackets and dipstick are held in place with small nuts and bolts. These disconnect easily with hand tools.

Also disconnect the brake booster vacuum hose from the manifold. This is another connection that is simply a press-on with a hose clamp. Take photos of everything to be sure that the hoses and valves and brackets return to their intended connections when you reassemble.

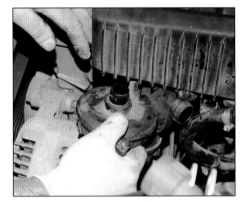

Unplug the various emissions control and engine management devices from the underside of the M52 manifold.

6 Remove the cam sensor wiring connection from the forward end of the fuel rail and then unplug the wiring harness connector at each fuel injector. Next, carefully separate the fuel rail and fuel injectors free from the manifold. Gently work the rail back and forth while lifting until it comes out of the casting. It is easy to bend or kink the fuel rail, so extreme caution should be used. Some penetrating oil or lubricant such as WD-40 can make this easier, especially if the injectors have been in place for many years or miles. Be prepared to renew the O-ring seals on the injectors.

Remove the fuel feed and return hoses. Again, take a photo or tag the hoses to make sure the correct connections are restored at reassembly time.

Spray the fuel rail with penetrating oil to help loosen the fuel injectors from the manifold.

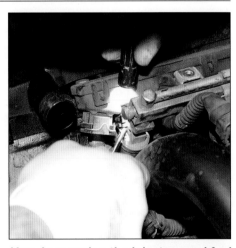

Here I am prying the injectors and fuel rail loose from the manifold. Be careful and take your time. Don't damage the fuel rail in any way.

This is the business end of a BMW fuel injector. To be sure you don't have any vacuum or fuel leaks, replace that gray O-ring seal before you put this injector into the new manifold.

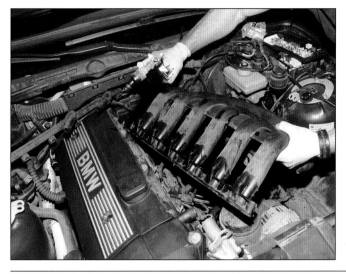

With all the nuts removed, you can just pull the manifold free of the engine.

7 Use a ratchet and socket with a long extension to remove the 11-mm nuts that hold the manifold to the engine. Be careful not to drop them on removal. The seven nuts include three that are somewhat hidden on the underside. When these are all removed, carefully work the manifold loose and lift it off the cylinder head. You can see that the manifold attaches very nearly vertically.

8 With the manifold off the car, turn it over and look at the underside. You see a base plate with many vacuum fittings attached to the manifold plenum with five Torx screws. Remove that plate from the manifold carefully. Also take a look at the underside of the M50 intake manifold and note that there is no corresponding plate. This is why you

need the adapter kit. The M50 manifold has a single central vacuum port, and the Turner adapter kit uses that port to distribute vacuum to all the stock devices, while bolting onto the manifold using the existing threaded fittings. The Turner kit is made from machined aluminum and is anodized to look good and protect the aluminum.

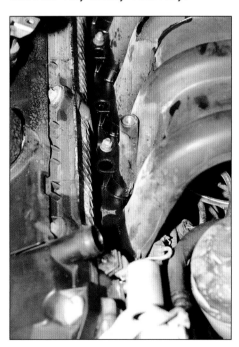

On the underside of the M52 manifold there is this emissions plate with all the connections on it. You remove this and put it onto the Turner Motorsports adapter device for the M50 manifold.

The manifold is held onto the head by these nuts and several that you can't see. Happily, the manifold fits over studs and is sealed with O-rings, so this is easier than you might expect.

You can see that there are far fewer connections on the underside of the M50 manifold on the left.

9 Using a fresh gasket from the kit, install the M52 base plate onto the Turner adapter, and then install the adapter onto the M50 manifold using the screws provided in the kit. A rubber O-ring on the adapter seals to the vacuum port on the M50 manifold. Plug all additional openings on the M50 manifold.

There is an electrical connection that must be removed and replaced with a press-in plug that is included in the Turner kit, and there is a small vacuum pipe that must be capped. The cap is also included in the kit.

10 Once the M52 plate and the adapter are installed on the M50 manifold reinstall the crankcase vent valve and the idle control valve. Note the pipes where you will reinstall the air pump solenoid, the fuel pressure regulator, and the purge valve.

Finally, reinstall the manifold support brackets in their original positions and orientation. If you are using the Turner kit, you need to drill two holes through the plastic support webs on the manifold. Consult the instructions that come with the Turner kit for details.

11 Some pieces must be extended or altered to work with the M50 manifold. For example, you have to extend the crankcase vent hose. The Turner kit comes with a heat-shrink extender for this purpose. Cut the hose as shown, and use a heat gun or a simple lighter to heat and shrink-fit the extender onto the part. You may choose to purchase a new crankcase vent hose if the existing part is old and likely to fail. Once extended, the hose fits the new manifold.

This hose must be lengthened to work with the M50 manifold. Turner's kit provides an extension, but you have to cut the hose and install the extension yourself.

The emissions plate transfers to the Turner Motorsports adaptor device and fits perfectly. This distributes the manifold vacuum as on the M52 manifold.

Cap and plug these ports on the M50 manifold, as they will not be used.

Cleaning the cut through the hose helps achieve a good seal when you install the extension.

Simply press the Turner adaptor into the M50 manifold. Threaded fasteners on the underside hold it in place.

With the Turner adaptor in place, the M50 manifold now accepts all the required connections from the M52 engine.

An extension is installed on the hose. The extension is a heat-shrink tubing, and a simple lighter or heat gun shrinks the extension tubing into place.

12 Completely clean the mating surface on the cylinder head to ensure a good seal with the O-rings on the manifold face. Replace all manifold O-ring gaskets and the O-ring around the throttle body mating surface before reinstalling.

Clean up the mating surface on the cylinder head before you attempt to install the M50 manifold. You want a good tight seal on all ports.

13 Position the new manifold in the engine. While it is loosely in place, reconnect the idle-control valve underneath. Then start the 11-mm manifold mounting nuts on their studs. These are small nuts and studs; they should be torqued to just 11 ft-lbs. Resist the temptation to tighten them, as the part is made of plastic and may deform. If you are concerned about backing out the nuts, use blue removable Lock-Tite on the threads.

14 Once the manifold has been secured, look at the mounting brackets and attach them to the engine. They may fit differently than they did with the M52 intake, so some adjustment may be required to accommodate the starter power cable, various hoses, and other parts. Once the brackets are secure, reattach the vacuum fittings to the underside of the manifold, including the purge valve, fuel pressure regulator, and the air pump solenoid connections. Install the modified crankcase vent hose now as well.

15 Install the fuel rail and injectors onto the new manifold. You simply place the fuel rail to the manifold and get it in place, then gently press each of the fuel injectors into place until they seat snugly. The rail may impact the mounting boss on the manifold in places, and some quick work with a file relieves that interference.

Next, install the adapter tabs that are part of the kit to align the M52 fuel rail with the M50 manifold threaded fittings. Reinstall the fuel intake and return lines according to the notes you made when you removed them.

Reinstall the camshaft sensor connection. Finally, reinstall the fuel injector harness fittings to the injectors and the oxygen sensor connections.

Press the fuel rail back into place after replacing the O-rings on the fuel injectors for a good seal.

16 When you install the throttle body, there is an adapter plate that must go between the throttle body and the intake manifold plenum. This is because the O-ring seal is placed on the throttle body on M52/S52 engines, and on the intake manifold plenum on M50/S50 engines. Replace both O-rings and use the adapter plate to ensure a perfect seal. Then connect the coolant lines back to the throttle body. Finally, reinstall the throttle position sensor to the top of the throttle body.

17 Reinstall the rest of the intake system, starting with the MAF tube and the stock or aftermarket intake system. Don't forget the alternator cooling duct and the cabin-air intake parts. You will find that the fuel rail cap does not fit correctly over the M50 manifold. You can modify it to fit, leave it off, let it fit poorly, or purchase a modified cap.

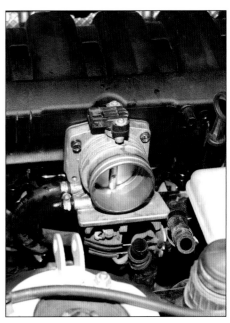

On the M50 manifold, the sealing O-ring is on the manifold. But on the M52, the O-ring is on the throttle body. Turner's kit bypasses this by using a thin metal plate to seal against both O-rings.

18 Reinstall the fuel pump fuse, recap the fuel filler, and reattach the battery. You may have to crank a few times and leave the ignition on for the fuel pump to refill the system, but the engine should start readily. You can check for vacuum leaks with a can of spray-on carburetor cleaner. Any vacuum leaks that suck air in from the engine bay cause the engine to stumble or rev a little

when hit with the carb cleaner spray. You may also see a check engine light if the leak is bad enough. Identify and isolate all leaks and repair them before driving.

Caution: You must also check the fuel rail and injectors for leaks. A leak in these components can spray atomized fuel into the engine bay and cause a catastrophic fire!

You should not expect to notice an immediate change in normal driving with the M50 intake manifold, because normal driving does not use wide open throttle at the high end of the RPM range very much. You need to take your car to a track day or a dyno session to really feel the difference.

Project Results

The results of this upgrade on the project 328i were truly impressive, yielding a gain of almost 20 peak horsepower with only moderate loss of torque across the whole curve and a substantial increase of torque and horsepower above 5,000 rpm.

Looking at the dyno graph by engine speed (RPM), the test with the M50 intake manifold installed is shown as the red line, while the prior test with the M52 manifold is in blue. You can see that the red line is slightly lower in both horsepower and torque until just above 5,000 rpm. Then the difference is dramatic, with horsepower continuing to climb until almost 6,000 rpm and torque remaining higher than with the M52 manifold. Both tests include the cold-air intake and the cat-back exhaust.

Consult the same dyno runs charted relative to wheel speed to see that horsepower and torque using the M50 manifold rise above 75 mph compared to the same engine running the M52 manifold. This manifold allows the project 328i to continue to accelerate when comparable cars are running out of breath on a long straightaway, while giving up very little at intermediate speeds.

The net result is that after seeing only nominal gains from the installation of the cold-air intake system

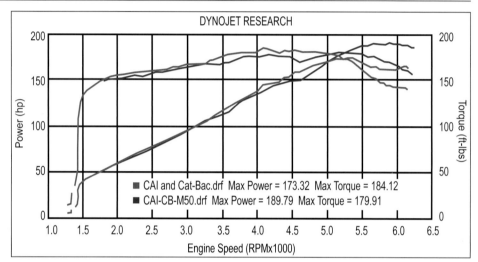

The M50 manifold swap has produced spectacular results. At just over 5,000 rpm, the horsepower and torque lines continue upward to redline, giving us a maximum horsepower reading of 189 and a max torque reading of 179. That's down a bit in maximum torque, but the line is much flatter at the high end.

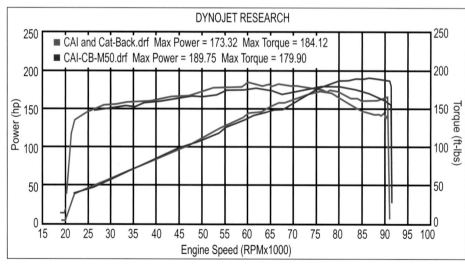

The same information charted by speed shows the benefit of the M50 manifold. Above 75 mph in fourth gear, the engine just keeps making more power instead of running out of air.

How to Reset the DME

When you make a change to the induction system, such as a new intake manifold or a new set of cams, you may want to completely reset the engine computer. It is not sufficient to simply disconnect the battery, because the DME carries its own capacitor to maintain its memory across such events. You will want to reset the DME.

To fully reset the DME, put the positive and negative battery terminals together for about half an hour. Remove the battery before you do this, so there's no danger of shorting out the system.

Follow These Steps

1 Disconnect both the positive and negative leads from the battery and remove the battery from the car completely.

2 Hold the positive and negative leads together with the clamps touching for 30 minutes. You can use a zip tie or spring clamp to hold the leads together. This allows the charge in the DME capacitor to drain off safely.

3 Reinstall the battery and reconnect the leads normally.

Caution: Do not bridge the battery terminals in any way, and do not touch the positive and negative leads together while the battery is installed. Catastrophic damage to your car will be the result.

and the cat-back exhaust, you have finally found and relieved one of the big choke points in the air-fuel flow of the engine. It is likely the case that without those two upgrades, the results of this intake manifold change would not have been so dramatic. This proves the point that you should make changes as a coordinated effort and all the parts should complement one another to increase power. Also note that this improvement did not require any change to the engine management software. I am still running BMW's software at this point.

To further maximize the effect of this manifold upgrade, you should consider additional upgrades, including M3 or aftermarket custom-profile performance cams, upgraded capacity fuel injectors, and perhaps a larger-mass airflow tube. However, any change to the MAF tube requires immediate custom software tuning, as the DME calculates air delivery based on the stock MAF tube. Some off-the-shelf software tunes are available for particular cam/MAF/fuel injector combinations.

Forced Induction

One of the decisions people make when selecting a car is whether to purchase a turbocharged, supercharged, or naturally aspirated model. In a naturally aspirated model, air and fuel is sucked through the air filter and into the combustion chambers through the motion of the piston while the intake valve is open. The vacuum generated by moving the pistons is the only action that pulls air into the combustion chamber.

In a turbocharged engine, exhaust gases are used to turn a compressor that pressurizes the air going into the combustion chambers. With a supercharger, the engine's crankshaft motion drives the compressor, usually with a toothed belt. A turbocharger or supercharger artificially forces a greater volume of air into the engine. A basic turbocharger or supercharger can boost typical air pressure by about 10 to 15 psi. The engine computer can then be modified to allocate more fuel, which results in more power to turn the engine.

Of course, turbocharged or supercharged engines are more complex than a naturally aspirated model, and they have more moving parts to break, and the engine works under greater stress and more extreme conditions. All that takes its toll

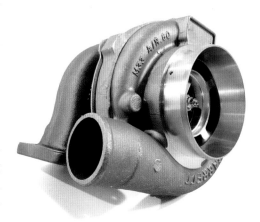

The turbocharger is often thought to be the best modification ever for making power. However, it's very expensive to install on an E36, and it puts substantial stress on the engine; the engine setup has to be ideally suited for the turbo. Some owners have blown up a few engines on the way to dialing it in.

Turbo Kits

A wide range of turbo kits is available for all makes and models on the market, but the actual manufacturers of turbo housings are IHI, Mitsubishi, and Garrett. You're not likely to find anything that's not based on those three brands of turbochargers. Kit builders add intake and exhaust parts as necessary, but the turbo itself is always a standard unit. For this reason, pay extra attention to the quality of manifolds and other parts included with a turbo kit if you choose to install one.

Always closely inspect the kit and buy only from reputable North American retailers. Turbo kits available online for $500 or $600 often simply cannot be made to work. Read the fine print on the eBay auction listings and you find that "all sales are final." There's a good reason for that.

Turbo Specialties is the leading manufacturer of kits for the E36, and they use high-quality Garrett turbos. The lowest you can expect to pay for a quality turbo kit is about $3,500 for the GT28R kit from Turbo Specialties, and prices range upward from there for more powerful kits. Various online retailers offer the exact same kits for the same price. Bear in mind that whatever kit you choose, you still have to pay for custom installation and engine tuning to achieve reliability and drivability.

This is a twin-scroll turbo turbine side. By using two differently shaped scrolls, the turbo spins up quickly at low RPM with less gas flow, and then stays spun up and strong at high RPM as well.

on reliability, especially when the engine was not designed for forced induction.

Alternatives to Forced Induction

All 6-cylinder E36 engines run either 10.2:1 or 10.5:1 compression. That's already a high-compression engine. Most engines designed for forced induction start at about 8.5:1 or even lower. This means that if you install a supercharger or turbocharger on your E36, you are able to set up only a few pounds of boost before you damage the engine. Exceeding about 6 pounds of boost is not a risk of damage although it's a certainty without proper engine management and tuning.

If you are starting with a 323, 325, or 328 engine, consider that you can generally purchase a good S50 or S52 engine along with all the installation parts you need for a fraction of the cost of any turbo or supercharger kit on the market, and you

This is a great shot of how a turbo works. On the left, exhaust gases drive the turbine wheel, and on the right the compressor wheel pulls in air and compresses it through the volute. In the center is the turbine shaft and bearings.

will probably get more usable power out of that swap. In addition, if you install one of these engines rather than a turbo or supercharger, you will experience more longevity and fewer installation and maintenance hassles. If you build a new engine to accommodate more boost, you're looking at replacement pistons and a full custom bottom-end build, which is even more expensive.

If you are starting with an M3 engine, S50 or S52, the stock compression ratio is 10.5:1. You can gain substantial horsepower from forced induction, up to 450 wheel horsepower and beyond, but the engine may not be durable enough to support that much horsepower. Bluntly, if you want a turbocharged BMW, your best value is to purchase a 2007–2010 335i, which comes from BMW already twin-turbocharged with 302 hp and 295 ft-lbs of torque. With this model, a simple software upgrade makes up to 380 hp. Apart from some fuel pump issues for which a factory recall already happened, these are quite reliable cars. An E36 engine with an aftermarket turbo is likely to be more expensive and less reliable than the newer car.

Turbochargers and Turbo Systems

As mentioned, turbochargers work by using exhaust gas flow to spin a turbine wheel, which sits on a spindle that also includes a compressor wheel on the other side of the turbo. The compressor wheel pushes air into the engine to help make more power by burning more fuel and air.

That's the simple version, but when you turbocharge an engine, there's a lot more to it. Not only do you have to regulate the boost pressure, but you want to choose the right turbo for the job. A small turbo builds boost quickly, but only to a limited level. A larger turbo can move more air when it's up to speed, but takes longer to spool up, creating turbo lag. A twin-scroll turbo balances the two by having both a small and a large "volute," the snail-shell shape in which the air flows.

Beyond the turbo unit itself, you need to install many different com-

This is the turbine wheel exposed. The compressor side is on the bottom.

The compressor wheel is shaped differently, to throw the air outward into the volute.

ponents in the intake and exhaust systems to accommodate the turbo. The exhaust system needs to be modified or replaced because the turbo generally mounts on or near the exhaust manifold. The exhaust path requires both a direct pipe through the turbine and an additional path coming from the turbo's waste gate.

Most people run larger 3- or 3½-inch exhaust systems on turbo cars to reduce backpressure at the turbine outlet. Reducing the backpressure at the turbine outlet makes it very easy to produce a higher pressure differential across the turbine. And when you do that, you accelerate turbine spool-up significantly. This allows the engine builder to install a larger turbocharger and still have quick spool-up and low-speed torque characteristics, and also achieve improved power performance from the mid-range on up to redline.

With a turbo you also have to redesign the intake path, from the fresh air collection and filtering, through the mass airflow sensor, to the turbo, and then to some kind of intercooler before routing the pressurized air to the intake manifold and the engine.

Intercoolers

When you compress air, it becomes hot. Hot air is not as good for combustion as cold air. Cold air is denser for any given volume, and more air means that more fuel can be allocated, which delivers more power. Also, hot intake charge temps can result in pre-ignition (detonation), which will damage the engine quickly, so it helps overall performance to cool the air after it has been compressed by the turbocharger and before it enters the engine. The intercooler cools the compressed air.

E36 turbo kits place the intercooler at the front of the car, because the increased air collection area and better rearward venting improve cooling efficiency. It's also the only place where there is space for an intercooler. E36 turbo kits place the intercooler in the vicinity of the front bumper, so a body kit may also be necessary.

The front-mounted location of the intercooler means there's a long path from the turbo to the intercooler and back to the intake manifold. There is perhaps a 10-foot column of air moving through that system at any given time, and it takes time to pressurize that much volume. This situation creates tremendous potential for pressure spikes when the throttle is shut off at full boost.

On the E36, the best place for an intercooler is below the front bumper. In fact, it's about the only place you can put it without a major hood modification.

Recirculation and Blow-Off Valves

After the intercooler, you also need a recirculation valve or a blow-off valve (BOV). If the engine management is based on a mass airflow (MAF) sensor, you must use a recirculating valve. MAF systems meter the air after the air filter but before the intake manifold, and the engine management systems allocate fuel based on the amount of air metered through the system. Thus, any air leak to atmosphere after the MAF sensor compromises the tuning of the car. If the turbo kit uses Alpha-N or a manifold absolute pressure (MAP) sensor exclusively, then a vent-to-atmosphere design of BOV can be used.

Blow-off or recirculation valves are necessary to relieve pressure when you lift off the gas, to avoid a reverse shock wave hitting the turbo and reducing turbine speed. As you increase boost and especially if you use a higher-rated turbocharger, you want to invest in a more capable BOV to protect the system from boost spikes. A bypass or recirculation valve is a related device that performs the same function as a BOV. The difference between the two is that most blow-off valves vent pressure to the outside atmosphere, while a bypass

This is an aftermarket vent-to-atmosphere blow-off valve. When pressure rises in the intake stream, this valve opens to let the air out.

All Turbos Need Blow-Off or Recirculation Valves

With a turbocharged engine, you have a tube full of compressed air about 10 feet long. This column of air is moving very fast, taking only a fraction of a second to make it from one end of that tube to the other. When you are at 7,500 rpm and you lift your foot off the throttle to shift, the throttle plate closes. Where does that air go? The column of air has to come to a complete stop, and a pressure wave bounces all the way back through the intercooler and back to the turbo. When that air hits the compressor wheel, it tries to twist the shaft and the blades on the turbocharger. The turbo will go from 110,000 to 120,000 rpm down to 10,000 rpm in an instant.

Then you shift into the next gear and apply wide open throttle, and suddenly the turbo has to accelerate from 10,000 rpm all the way back up to 110,000 rpm again. You feel that process as turbo lag. With a very high-capacity blow-off valve in the system, that air doesn't just stop, and it doesn't cause the turbocharger to lose 100,000 rpm of shaft speed more or less instantaneously. Because air can exit the blow-off valve, the turbocharger conserves its shaft speed. Recovering boost pressure after a shift is much more rapid if you use an appropriate blow-off valve.

valve routes the released air back into the intake stream after the MAF, but before the turbo.

On a street car, you probably prefer to maintain strict air/fuel ratios and a smooth idle. For that application, you want to use a fully recirculated valve. An aftermarket recirculating valve allows you to change the volume of recirculated air and the spring tension that controls when the valve activates. For racing, or if you just like a nice racing sound, a vented-to-atmosphere valve gives you the distinctive venting whistle you hear when a performance turbo car shifts gears. But do not do this at the expense of the engine tuning if you are running a MAF-based engine management system.

Waste Gates

Waste gates are a part of turbocharging that many people misunderstand. They often confuse the waste gate function with the blow-off valve function. A waste gate senses when full boost has been achieved, and then opens to allow exhaust gases to bypass the turbine wheel. Where the

blow-off valve is used on the intake side, the waste gate works entirely on the exhaust side.

A lot of people think that running high boost means the turbo needs a big waste gate. In fact, as boost level

This is a waste gate on top, and a turbine wheel at the bottom. When more exhaust gas is produced than the turbo can use, the waste gate opens and lets that excess gas bypass the turbo and pass through the exhaust stream.

rises, the amount of exhaust gas that needs to be routed around the turbo is reduced. Those engines need to run most of the available exhaust gas through the turbine to maintain more than 100,000 rpm on the turbo shaft. For almost all purposes, the waste gate designed into the turbo unit is more than sufficient.

Manual Boost Controllers

Manual boost controllers can be used to coax a little more boost out of a turbocharger. But be aware that boost levels are generally controlled through the DME, and a reflash or DME upgrade should really be your first choice for modest increases in boost pressure because the DME also remaps the fuel program and ignition at the same time, maintaining balance.

Manual boost controllers within reach of the driver are engine killers. Because we're human and we're

doing all this work to go fast, it's almost impossible to resist the temptation to reach over and dial up just a little more boost. The car responds with more power, so you dial up a little more. It works right up to the moment that something in the engine breaks, usually with spectacularly bad results.

Other Turbo Upgrades

The further you take a turbo upgrade, the more you're going to need to modify. For example, you will likely have to replace the factory fuel injectors with larger units that flow enough fuel to keep up with the amount of air moving through the system.

Finally, you need to tune the DME, and that requires professional work. Most people are unable to achieve a software or programming solution to a newly turbocharged

Some cars have water spray that can be directed at the intercooler. The evaporative effect helps the intercooler cool the compressed air better.

engine. That solution is either going to come from a standalone computer or a reprogramming of the factory computer.

About Supercharger Systems

In almost every respect, a supercharger system faces the same issues as a turbocharger system. You still have to plan for an intercooler and a recirculation or blow-off valve, new DME programming is required, and you might need larger fuel injectors. But a supercharger does not require you to redesign the exhaust system. The tradeoff is that you have to run a new belt off the crankshaft to drive the blower.

The same considerations for boost levels apply to superchargers as to turbos. You cannot exceed the capacity of the engine to handle the relative compression increase delivered by the blower, or you will blow up the engine very quickly.

Several internal designs for superchargers include twin screw, Roots type, and centrifugal, but none are really better than any others. What matters is the overall quality of the supercharger kit. Look for the installation parts and how well the kit seems to be integrated with the stock engine.

It goes without saying that "superchargers" based on electric fans or other designs are worthless.

You have to exercise discretion with this. A boost controller allows you to change the settings for the turbo to give you more power at the touch of a button. It's dangerous because it's so tempting to keep pressing that button. You have more power right up to the point at which the engine blows up.

When you move up to forced induction, you may need to move up to larger fuel injectors, a bigger fuel rail, and a more powerful fuel pump. But the stock setup should be fine if you don't use a turbo or supercharger.

When it comes to selecting a supercharger for the E36, you get what you pay for, and to achieve meaningful and reliable performance, you can choose from several reputable systems. Active Autowerks is the most popular supercharger system on the market, and the Stage 2 kit for the M3 can cost more than $10,000, while the Stage 2 kit for the 328i costs about $6,000. Stage 1 kits from Active Autowerks cost about $5,000, not including installation and tuning. Other supercharger kits such as VF Engineering also cost about $5,000.

Remember, all aftermarket forced induction systems require custom installation to achieve good fit and finish, and all require custom engine tuning to achieve reliability and drivability. It is possible to sort out a forced induction setup, but it takes some work.

Getting Fuel into the Engine

The stock E36 fueling system is based on the engine management map of the stock E36. There is enough adjustability in the system to improve output with intake and exhaust upgrades, but once you start changing cams or adding a turbo or supercharger and flow substantially more air through the engine, you also need to upgrade your ability to feed fuel. This can mean changing the injectors as well as the DME programming and possibly the fuel pump. The engine tuner should tell you when improving fuel flow is necessary, and many aftermarket products also include information about necessary fuel flow requirements.

Fuel Pumps and Injectors

Among the upgrades to an E36 fueling system, the first stage in get-

ting gasoline from the tank to the engine is the fuel pump. In a performance engine, the stock pump may not flow enough fuel to keep pressure up. Aftermarket fuel pumps and pressure regulators are readily available to provide adequate fuel to the components down the line.

The fuel arrives at the injectors, which are valved jets that squirt a measured amount of fuel into each cylinder according to timing and volume instructions from the DME. Injectors are rated according to the amount of fuel they can inject into the intake stream, and this measurement is expressed in pounds. BMW is unusual in using pounds instead of cubic centimeters. Stock E36 fuel

This is a basic BMW pink-top fuel injector, rated at 21.5 pounds per hour at 3.5 bars of fuel pressure. It is standard on E36, M3, and 328i cars and is sufficient for any normally aspirated E36.

pressure is 3.5 bars; the injector capacity is based on that pressure.

BMW injectors are identified by color to represent their capacity in pounds per hour. Green-top injectors are rated at 17.5 pounds and came on 1992–1995 cars; pink-top injectors are rated at 21.5 pounds and came on 1996–1999 cars, including the S52 M3. Blue-top injectors are 24 pounds, and generally used with forced induction on E36 cars. To make matters a little confusing, green-tops are rated at 42 pounds for advanced forced-induction systems.

Most engine modifications made to allow more air to flow through the engine (cold-air intake, M50 intake manifold, performance exhaust header, high-flow catalyst or cat-delete, and cat-back exhaust) do not need larger injectors. Forced induction systems often require both injector and fuel delivery upgrades.

Engine Management and DME Upgrades

In an older car, mechanical parts controlled fuel delivery and ignition. With the E36 and other modern cars,

Fuel System Requirements and Cleanliness

Whenever you work on the fuel injectors and the fuel injection system, you need to realize that this system depends on absolute cleanliness and perfect sealing. You should always work on this system in a clean environment and use new seals every time you remove the injectors from your car. A damaged seal, a poorly lubricated seal, or a small piece of foreign matter in the injector area can cause a high-pressure fuel or air leak into the engine, with disastrous consequences.

all those functions are performed by the digital motor electronics (DME) also sometimes known as the engine (or electronic) control unit, the engine management system, the "chip," or the computer. The DME controls the timing and force of the spark, typically with individual coils for each spark plug. The DME also controls the amount and timing of fuel delivery through the fuel injection system, and it controls the amount of boost pressure from the turbocharger. The DME almost always includes a top speed and maximum RPM governor.

The DME is the car's brain, and it operates using input from various sensors throughout the intake, combustion, and exhaust systems. It adjusts mixture and timing based on indications of the air density coming into the engine, combustion performance, and exhaust gas composition and temperature. In cars with traction control, the DME may take input from the brakes or differentials to detect a loss of traction and respond by making changes to reduce torque to get the car back under control. Stability control functions are primarily controlled by the antilock brake system (ABS) computer in conjunction with a number of sensors such as brake pressure, wheel speed, and yaw rate. When it comes to stability, the DME is a reactive system, taking orders from the ABS computer.

Most 1996 and later OBD II–compliant DME computers use "flash" memory (similar to the re-writable memory chip in a digital camera or thumb drive). Information is retained in the memory even if you completely disconnect its power source.

When an automaker builds a car, they play it safe with the DME programming. They need to meet emissions standards, fuel economy standards, and perhaps most important, longevity standards for their products. So they program the DME to accept whatever kind of fuel their cars may have to drink, a wide range of altitudes at which the cars may have to operate, and a big safety margin to keep the engines from blowing up.

Obviously then, the DME is an excellent place to find some more performance. With naturally aspirated engines like those found in E36 series cars, gains are incremental. You're playing with spark advance and fuel delivery curves. Cars that feature forced induction can gain more power through DME tuning that raises boost levels, but for the E36 that means going with a standalone DME replacement.

DME programming is complex, and the vast majority of us are not qualified to tinker with it. Many products on the market have proven programs that optimize your car's performance with the specific hardware modifications you have made.

Vendors with DME software solutions include Turner Motorsports, Dinan, and Conforti. None of them have really spectacular results by themselves and are only recommended when doing a substantial number of upgrades such as a European High-Flow MAF or throttle body, M3 cams, M50 intake manifold, and so on.

Legal Issues and the DME

When changing the DME, you need to consider the following: It's an emissions control device and covered under the same federal law that governs the catalytic converters. Therefore, it's against federal law to tamper with an emissions control device in any way on a car that is registered and driven on the public roads. These upgrades should be considered for dedicated track cars only.

Standalone Engine Management Systems

Standalone engine management systems allow real-time full programming of every aspect of the engine's performance. You have complete control over anything and everything. The downside is that standalone engine management systems are very difficult to program because you have to program everything. You really need to know what you're doing. You have to know the software very well, and you need to know what that motor's asking you for in terms of crank, cold start, hot start, everything. They usually come with a base map that has some of that stuff figured out for you. Usually with a standalone, a professional programmer can spend a day or even a week with the car to make it just right. If you put standalone in your own car, you're probably going to spend a year. The factory spent millions of dollars for everything to start and be smooth and perfect. A standalone engine management system has the most flexibility to help you make power, as well as the ability to do multiple maps for different conditions, but it's also the most difficult to work with.

Also, many standalones have no OBD-II or emissions information. If you have to pass emissions tests by reading the computer codes, they might not be there. The standalone is definitely the best choice for a race car that doesn't have to pass emissions tests, but less practical for a street-driven car.

IMPROVING ENGINE INTERNALS

With any E36 model, or any other engine for that matter, there is only so far you can go with enhancing performance before you overstress the core of the engine: the valves, pistons, connecting rods, crankshaft, bearings, and the engine block itself. With the M50 and M52 engines, you can do as much as possible with intake and exhaust and never come

Accessing the inside of the engine generally means big expense. Unless you're looking to use forced induction to develop a lot more horsepower and torque than the engine was designed to handle, the bottom end of an E36 engine is strong enough to handle anything you want to do.

close to stressing the core engine components with your changes, and you can take things quite a ways into the world of forced induction before you need to think about digging into the engine below the cams.

For the purposes of this book, engine "internal" components means anything underneath the cam cover and above the oil pan, generally known as the long-block. I cover cam upgrades with a step-by-step project and take a good look at a car that has been through several different core engine development options on its way to more than 700 wheel horsepower.

The Long Block

It's important to remember that whenever you modify on the long block, you're changing the design that the BMW factory engineers

tested, developed, and made reliable. You are likely introducing new parts, or changing the relationship of the parts that are already there, and the results of that process are never as well understood as the BMW factory understands the way a stock engine works.

First, the engine is a system, and changing any part of that system (from piston design to the block deck height to the bore or stroke) places different stresses on other parts of the system. If you change the compression ratio or the length of the stroke, you may find that the connecting rods tend to fail. The trouble is, it's expensive to learn that lesson, and there are few guarantees when you're building a custom engine.

The best advice is to keep the performance modifications within the envelope that the stock long block can support. That results in at least 400 hp or even more. Beyond that, be patient with the process and get the best advice you can about how to build the bottom end to survive the amount of power you want to put down.

The following sections look at each major part of the E36 engine, and offer observations from experts and experienced owners.

Camshaft Selection

By far the easiest upgrade to engine internals is in the camshafts. There are two of them on every E36, and they sit right on top of the engine and all you have to do is remove the cam cover to access them. You have several good options for upgrades here.

Your easiest option is to install the cams from an E36 M3 that matches your car's year. That is, 1995 and older E36 cars should use the cams from a 1995 M3 with the S50 engine. The 1996 and later cars with single VANOS should use the M3 cams from a 1996–1999 M3 with the S52 engine.

Aftermarket cams generally start out pretty close to the specs on the M3 cams. Schrick sells a set of cams that are made to the M3 specifications (intake 252 degrees, 10.2 mm of lift, exhaust 244 degrees, 9.5 mm of lift), or you can go with a much more aggressive Schrick cam that boosts intake duration to 264 degrees and 11.2 mm of lift and exhaust duration to 256 degrees and 10.6 mm of lift. But be aware that this cam requires you to change fuel injectors, deliver more intake air to the engine, and reprogram the DME.

Similarly, a few racing cams are available, and several online retailers carry Sunbelt Racing Engines camshafts. These should be used only in custom-built racing applications because they are not likely to be tractable enough for day-to-day street use.

If you are planning to build a completely custom engine, talk to your engine builder about selecting the right camshaft. Custom engines have different clearances between the valves and the piston faces at top dead center, and you have to be sure that the engine design won't result in valve-piston contact. Custom engine builders often machine the top of the engine block to smooth it and increase compression, and that's what changes the spacing between valves and pistons. If you put a high-lift cam in place, you have to be sure it works.

Another option is to custom-grind your own cams, and many shops can do this. But choosing duration and lift and timing are generally tasks for accomplished mechanical engineers.

How Camshafts Work

Cams do their work by opening the valves a precise amount (called *lift*) for a precise amount of time (called *duration*) at a precise time in the engine's rotational cycle (called *valve timing*). When the valve opens earlier, it's called *advance*. When it opens later, it's *retard*. Your E36 engine has two intake and two exhaust valves per cylinder. With most engines, including the E36, there is a period of time when both the intake and exhaust valves are slightly open, and this is known as *overlap*. The overlap occurs just before the exhaust valve closes on the upward exhaust stroke and just before the intake valve opens for the downward intake stroke.

By changing the shape and size of the cam lobes, and by changing the amount of overlap, you can change the running characteristics of any engine. Lift and duration are functions of the size and shape

Camshaft profiles have a lot to do with how the engine performs, but it turns out that changing cams doesn't have a big effect on usable performance.

of the cam lobe. More lift (within limits) means the valve opens farther and more mixture can flow through. It's possible to go too far because all E36 engines are "interference" designs where the pistons may hit the valves if the cams are too tall and not timed correctly. Plus, you need tougher valvesprings to run an extremely high-lift cam; they have to pull the valve back farther and faster. Tougher valvesprings also put more wear on the tappets and the cam lobes.

Longer duration means the valve is open longer and more mixture can flow through, again within limits. Longer duration cams offer great high-end power because they offer more time to put more mixture into the cylinder, but they do that at the expense of smooth running at low RPM. Long duration cams also run into limits because of piston interference. With all of that going on, you should generally stick to an M3 or one of the few aftermarket cams designed for a high-performance street car.

However, overlap is where some gains may be made. On single overhead cam engines, both the exhaust and intake cam lobes are on the same shaft. This means that overlap is built into the cam when it is made and is always fixed. But on twin cam engines like the E36 line, you can alter the overlap by changing the relationship of the cams to each other.

At idle and low engine speeds, it's best to retard the intake cam so as not to have any overlap. This helps the engine idle smoothly and stops exhaust and intake charges from mixing. But as the engine throttle opens and the engine spins up, it's helpful to advance the intake cam a little bit to more completely fill the cylinder with air-fuel mixture. Also, advancing the intake cam means that the intake valves close earlier, before the piston starts up on the compression stroke. This helps achieve the maximum compression on the charge.

Lots of good things happen when you the intake valves close before bottom dead center, including more power over the fat part of the band, better fuel economy, and reduced emissions through more complete combustion. All that happens when the cam is advanced in the mid-range.

However, at the higher end of the engine's RPM range, there isn't enough time to fill the cylinder completely, so the engine starts to run out of breath. At the high end, you want to retard the cam a little bit again for the greatest possible amount of mixture into the cylinder. So you can see that with fixed cam timing, there is a tradeoff between mid-range torque and high-end horsepower.

Tip: E36 engines are extremely sensitive to vacuum leaks. The plastic valvecovers tend to crack with age, and the valvecover gaskets harden in place. Always replace all exposed gaskets and O-rings when working with the cams or VANOS system to avoid vacuum leaks.

The VANOS System

BMW effectively cheats the cam timing tradeoff between mid-range torque and high-end horsepower with a system called VANOS. The name derives from the English and German words VAriable NOckenwellen Steuerung (or variable camshafts control). BMW started putting VANOS on its engines late in the 1992 model year. The first, or single, VANOS operated only on the intake camshaft and was either fully actuated or not actuated. This is the VANOS that you find on all U.S. market E36 models from the 1993 model year onward.

The double VANOS system was introduced with the E46 line. In contrast to the E36 VANOS, the double VANOS adjusts timing on both camshafts and is infinitely variable within its operating parameters. This is to say that where an E36 VANOS is simply all the way advanced or all the way retarded, the E46 VANOS is smooth and varied in its operation.

Single VANOS boosts performance by automatically advancing the intake cam as the engine speed rises off idle up to about 4,400 rpm and then retards the cam again from 4,400 rpm onward. This action primarily enhances mid-range fuel economy and helps with emissions, but also helps with mid-range power. Retarding the intake cam again at the high end helps make power at the high end of the RPM range.

The VANOS system is hydraulically controlled. By manipulating oil pressure on either side of a piston in a cylinder, the VANOS system moves the piston forward or backward in relation to the engine. The piston is connected to a shaft that has helical grooves cut into it. The intake camshaft drive sprocket has opposing helical grooves so that when the VANOS piston moves the shaft forward and back, the helical grooves slide together and rotate the intake cam relative to the exhaust cam. This advances or retards the relative cam timing between the two.

Project: Freshening the VANOS System

Over time the seals that operate the VANOS cam timing system deteriorate and begin to leak, changing the oil-pressure balance that actuates the VANOS system. Also, the bushings in the VANOS tend to wear, and that can make the VANOS system rattle. Beisan Systems has repair kits that eliminate both of these problems, and for a few dollars more they deliver a set of specialty tools that make the repair much easier and safer for the parts. The entire kit, with tools, costs about $80, compared to rebuilt VANOS assemblies selling at more than $250.

You can find detailed instructions for both the seal replacement and the rattle repair at beisansystems.com, but I installed both Beisan kits myself in an afternoon. Beisan recommends doing these projects together, which makes sense because you have the system apart in either case.

To complete this project you need the VANOS seals kit, the anti-rattle kit, and the special VANOS tools sold by Beisan. You should also plan to replace the valvecover gasket and VANOS gasket at the same time. Replacing the washers that hold the VANOS banjo bolt in place is also necessary. You need some coolant, as you remove the radiator tank to access the VANOS area.

You also need several BMW special tools in addition to a full tool set of your own. These include cam blocks, a crankshaft lock pin, sprocket turning tool, and a camshaft tensioner lock pin.

Tip: Consider that if you plan to upgrade the camshafts (as described later in this chapter) this is a good time to do both jobs. You have to disassemble all this anyway to replace the cams.

This project was performed on the project 1996 328i with the M52 engine. Beisan Systems has a detailed procedure for both M50TU and M52 engines on their website, but here are some general procedures.

Follow These Steps

1 Remove the valvecover, the engine fan, and the radiator shroud and tank. Refer to the shop manual for specific instructions. You need to remove the ignition coils and spark plugs, and all their related hardware. Remove the intake cam cover as well.

If your car has more than about 80,000 miles on the odometer, you need to remove and rebuild the VANOS system.

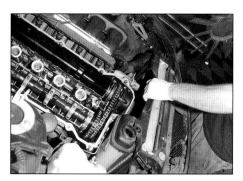

You have to remove the whole radiator to access the VANOS. There's no fast way to do this. Remove all the hoses and connections and be careful as you lift it out. If the radiator is older, maybe now is the time to install a new replacement radiator and hoses.

2 Using a 22-mm socket on the crankshaft pulley, turn the engine until the no. 1 (forward) cylinder is at top dead center. You know when this has happened because the cam lobes for that cylinder are pointing toward each other at a 45-degree angle. Notice the timing mark on the crankshaft harmonic balancer and on the timing cover. Also notice that the square castings on the rear ends of the camshafts are even with the valvecover mating surface on the head casting.

Remove the rear-most valvecover studs and install the BMW cam blocks on the square ends to lock the cams in position. You might have to wiggle the cams a bit to make the block fit; use a 24-mm wrench on the hex shape cast into the middle of each camshaft. Also place the crankshaft locking pin in place in the hole near the starter motor from the underside of the engine. There is a plug you must remove.

The cam block is a special tool that holds the cams in position while you work. This is a critical tool so do not attempt any work around the cams without one of these.

This is a BMW crank lock pin. It is used to pin the crankshaft into position with the no. 1 cylinder at top dead center.

3 Remove the VANOS oil hose and 19-mm banjo bolt. Remove the 13-mm VANOS intake solenoid bolts, noting that the top bolt secures the engine lift bracket. Unplug the VANOS solenoid electrical cable. Remove the two 10-mm nuts that secure a vacuum pipe to the engine. Also remove the 19-mm exhaust sprocket access plugs from the VANOS front plate.

You must detach the banjo bolt and fitting that delivers oil pressure to the VANOS system. Put a rag underneath the fitting because there will be some drips.

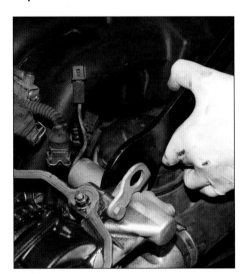

A large wrench is required to remove the solenoid that actuates the VANOS system.

Removing these two plugs allows you to access the bottom two nuts that hold the intake cam chain sprocket onto the end of the exhaust cam.

The VANOS solenoid and oil supply banjo bolt. These parts can be safely reused.

4 Look at the valve chains for a moment. A primary valve chain comes up from the crankshaft to drive the exhaust cam, and then a secondary chain drives the intake cam. Undo the four E10 Torx bolts that hold the sprocket assembly together. You need to remove those access plugs to remove the bottom bolts. Then press down on the top chain tensioner and place the retaining pin up to the chain, but not under it!

Tip: Put a rag underneath the sprocket area in case you drop a bolt. Be careful!

You can see the chain tensioner in the center of the photo, with the retainer pin holding pressure on the internal spring. Don't release it without a chain there.

5 Remove the rest of the 10-mm nuts that secure the VANOS assembly front plate to the engine. Put another rag under the VANOS area to catch excess oil. Now work the VANOS assembly away from the intake cam and the engine. Remember that the VANOS uses helical cut gears, so you have to wiggle things a little bit to remove the assembly from the engine.

You have to wiggle the VANOS out because you need to disengage the helical gear that turns the cam to change the timing.

6 Working on your bench, undo the five 10-mm bolts that hold the VANOS assembly together. Remove the VANOS piston and gear assembly with its flange.

You first install the anti-rattle kit, which is a replacement bearing. Be sure you have the Beisan special socket and the vise jaw pads for this job. Clamp the piston and flange snugly (but not too tight!) in the vise with the pads in place. Orient the flange so that the raised bolt hole rests on the vise pad.

On the opposite end from the gear, you'll find a plug with a shallow 18-mm bolt head cast into its surface. Use the special socket to free it, but don't remove it yet. Take the assembly out of the vise and replace it with the gear in the vise so the plug is on top.

The VANOS gear has helical gears on the inside and outside faces. This is because the VANOS gear moves in and out. As it moves, the helical cut of the gear slightly rotates the intake cam to change the valve timing.

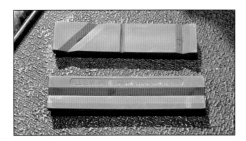

These plastic pads have magnets on the back. Place them in the bench vise to prevent damage to the VANOS components while you work.

7 Once the plug is on top, unthread the plug and remove it. Under it, you see the top of a Torx bolt and a bearing washer. Remove the bearing washer with a magnet and you see the roller bearing. Remove the roller bearing with the magnet. Set these in order on your workbench so they are sure to go back together in the same order and in the same orientation.

Remove the Torx bolt with a T30 Torx bit. This bolt uses a left-hand (reverse) thread, so turn it clockwise to loosen. Then remove the middle washer with the magnet and the second roller bearing beneath the washer. You can now remove the piston from the flange and gear.

Carefully work the outer bearing out of the piston; this is the part that is replaced with the bearing from the anti-rattle kit. There is one more washer to remove underneath the bearing.

With the piston and gear and bearing assembly removed, the VANOS shell can be cleaned.

Once the plug is removed, you can remove this Torx head bolt to access the bearings in the VANOS.

You can see the piston with its seal toward the bottom of the assembly and the VANOS gear at the top.

Place the VANOS assembly in the vise, using the protective vise inserts from Beisan Systems.

Beisan Systems also provides this machined socket to remove the plug to gain access to the bearings.

8 Clean all the parts, but keep them in order and orientation. Then reassemble with the new Beisan bearing. The torque spec on the Torx bolt is 6 ft-lbs. Once the bolt is torqued, loosen the vise and let the gear fall so you can center the second bearing. Hand-tighten the cap and reorient the assembly so the vise holds the mounting flange. Tighten the cap to 30 ft-lbs with the Beisan socket. You should be able to move the gear in and out, with just a little play in the shaft.

The Beisan Systems anti-rattle kit is this bushing, which restores proper bearing clearance. Replace the old worn bushing with this new one.

As you disassemble the VANOS bearing stack, place the parts in line so that you are sure to put them back together in the same way.

Reassemble and torque the VANOS assembly to proper specifications. Not too tight.

Stock Cams for the E36

Many different cams were installed on E36 6-cylinder models, mostly depending on whether the car was equipped with VANOS and whether the car is an M3. All E36 engines in North America made in 1993 or later use single VANOS on the intake cam, and some late 1992 cars are said to have the system as well.

The table below has the specifications for all stock BMW cams used in 6-cylinder E36 engines:

CAM	Duration (degrees)	Lift (mm)
M50 (Non-VANOS) Intake	240	9.7
M50 (Non-VANOS) Exhaust	228	9.7
M50TU/M52 Intake	228	9.0
M50TU/M52 Exhaust	228	9.0
S50 Intake	252	10.2
S50 Exhaust	244	9.5
S52 Intake	252	10.2
S52 Exhaust	244	9.7

You can see that the early 1992 M50 cams from before the VANOS era have more lift and the intake cam offers a longer duration than the M50TU/M52 cams offered from 1993 onward. The S50 cams offered in the 1995 M3 are also more aggressive than the M52 cams and differ only slightly from the later S52 cams used on the M3 from 1996 onward.

Because VANOS requires a specific cam design, you cannot put the early M50 intake cam on any VANOS engine on the intake side. But you can put the M50 intake cam on the exhaust side of an early M50 or an M50TU/M52 engine if you also transfer over the cam tray, and this is a popular modification for the pre-VANOS cars. However, you have several challenges to overcome with this plan, including the fact that the cams must be hand-timed with this modification, and errors can lead to catastrophic engine failure.

With VANOS-equipped M50TU/M52 engines, the best and easiest upgrade is to install a set of S50 or S52 cams from an M3.

9 Freshen the seals. Locate the Teflon ring around the perimeter of the piston. You can cut the old ring with a razor blade to facilitate removal. A rubber O-ring is underneath the Teflon sealing ring. Cut that, too, and remove it. You can now clean the VANOS piston.

Put the new O-ring in carefully so it does not twist, and then install the new Teflon sealing ring. Warm it in hot water if it's cold outside when you're working, but dry it before installation.

Part of the VANOS rebuild involves installing this rubber O-ring and Teflon sealing ring. These install in the circumferential groove around the piston to give a good oil pressure seal.

With the new O-ring and Teflon sealing ring, the VANOS piston is ready to be reassembled.

10 Apply some assembly lube to the VANOS cylinder wall and reassemble the piston and cylinder carefully so that the Teflon seal

makes good contact and is not pinched. Let it sit a couple of minutes and remove it again to help resize the seal. Now reassemble the piston and cylinder and reinstall the bolts.

Carefully put the VANOS piston back in the VANOS housing without damaging the Teflon sealing ring in any way. It's not difficult to do if you're careful about it. There's no trick to this; just be careful.

11 Reinstall the VANOS with a new gasket and reassemble the engine. If you are replacing the cams at the same time as this project, reinstall the VANOS when the new cams are in place. Drive the engine carefully for the next 100 miles or so to allow the VANOS to break in.

Project: Installing S52 M3 Cams

This project installs a set of used S52 cams from an M3 into the project 328i M52 engine. This engine has already been modified with the M50 intake manifold, cold-air intake system, and cat-back exhaust.

Follow These Steps

1 Follow the procedures in your shop manual and Steps 1–5 in "Project: Freshen the VANOS System."

Remove the valvecover, the engine fan, and the radiator shroud and tank. You need to remove the ignition coils and spark plugs, and all their related hardware. Remove the intake cam cover as well, and block the cams. Set the crankshaft pin. Remove the VANOS hardware.

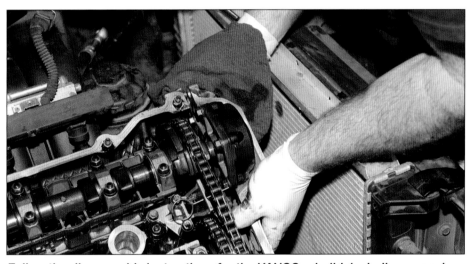

Follow the disassembly instructions for the VANOS rebuild, including removing the valvecover and disconnecting the timing chains and their sprockets. Finally, remove the cylinder head front plate.

You also have to remove the intake cam cover to access the intake cam.

2 With the VANOS removed, you can remove the intake cam timing chain. A diaphragm spring resides underneath a plate and three 10-mm nuts hold the plate onto the front of the intake camshaft. Remove these nuts and set them aside. Mark the intake cam sprocket at 12 o'clock for reference. Then remove the intake camshaft chain and sprockets as one assembly and keep the sprockets on the chain and oriented to each other.

Push the chain tensioner retainer all the way across the spring-loaded tensioner, then remove the 10-mm bolts that hold the tensioner in place and remove the tensioner as a unit.

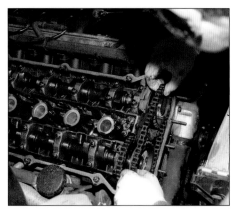

Remove both gears and the timing chain together. Keep them in their orientation to one another and replace them the same way.

You can see the intake cam has similar helical-cut gears to accept the VANOS gear. When the VANOS gear moves in and out, the helical cut to these gears rotates the cam to change its timing.

Push down on the intake cam chain to compress the tensioner, then insert the pin to hold the tensioner down.

3 Hold the cam timing chain tight so it stays in the teeth of the crankshaft end and does not allow the main timing chain tensioner to come undone, and wiggle the exhaust cam sprocket off the camshaft. Use a bungee cord or other means to keep the cam timing chain in place on the crankshaft end. Then undo the nuts on the bearing caps for the cams.

Replace the exhaust cam first. When the caps are all undone, remove them in order and keep track of the order. Put some assembly lube on the new cam bearing surfaces and place the new cam in the tray.

Make sure the cam installs with the lobes in the same orientation as the old one. The cam block helps you with this. Replace the bearing caps and torque to 11 ft-lbs.

Once the exhaust cam is in place, replace the exhaust cam sprocket and the timing chain. The bolt holes in the end of the cam should align with the left end of the elongated sprocket holes at this point.

Use a bungee cord hooked to the engine bay hood to suspend the main cam chain and keep it on its cog down at the crankshaft end.

Looking at these cams, you can see the M52 cam on the left and the much larger and fatter lobes of the S52 cam on the right.

Install the new cam in the same orientation as the old one. The special BMW cam block tool helps you do this right. If you don't have a cam tool, buy one immediately because the consequence of misaligning the camshafts is serious damage to the valves and pistons.

The sprocket should be aligned with the threaded bolt holes to the left sides of the slotted sprocket holes. These will be resolved back to center before you torque the sprocket into place.

4 Install the intake camshaft, maintaining its orientation with respect to the lobe positions. The cam end is square and the cam block holds it firmly. If you simply orient the new cam so the lobes are about where the old cam lobes were, the cam block adjusts the new cam to the proper orientation. Once again, the bearing cap nuts must be torqued at 11 ft-lbs.

Replace the chain tensioner and the intake timing chain sprockets, then the diaphragm spring and the cover plate.

Tip: It's a good idea to replace the cam chain tensioner and rebuild the VANOS system during this project. They do wear out.

All cams that fit the E36 have a square on the backside, and the cam block holds that square. Both cams are aligned with these squares and the edge of the cylinder head when they are in the correct positions.

5 It's time to reinstall the VANOS. Remove the old gasket and place a fresh VANOS gasket on the studs before you start. You have not yet put the bolts into the exhaust cam sprocket, so the intake timing chain and sprockets turn freely. You need to turn them a little to seat the helical gears of the VANOS system properly. Turn the exhaust sprockets a little clockwise until the first available tooth engages, then engage the helical gears and turn the sprockets counterclockwise again to work the VANOS into place.

Replace the intake cam timing chain and the VANOS assembly. This pulls the exhaust cam sprocket into place, and you can replace the bolts that hold the exhaust side sprockets together.

6 Now you can reinstall the sprocket bolts and reassemble the engine. Consult your shop manual to confirm all torque specs and procedures. When you have the cam timing system reassembled, remove the cam blocks and the crankshaft pin. Then use a socket on the crankshaft pulley to carefully turn the engine through several rotations, just to be sure that there's no valve to piston contact. If you encounter resistance, stop immediately and ensure that the cam timing is correct.

With the engine reassembled, leave the spark plugs out and remove the fuel pump fuse, then crank the engine with the starter motor until oil pressure is up and the VANOS has had a chance to fill with oil. This also helps lubricate the cams and seat them properly.

When this is done, complete the reassembly and test-fire the engine. Drive the engine carefully for the next 100 miles or so to allow the VANOS and cams to break in.

Project Results

I had high hopes and some concerns about the results of this project. The M3 cams used on the S52 engine offer substantially higher lift and duration than the stock M52 cams. With extra breathing room, I knew I'd be getting more air into the cylinders and I was concerned that the stock fuel injectors might not be able to supply enough fuel The M52 engine in the 328i uses pink-topped injectors, which flow 19 pounds at 3 bars of fuel pressure, and about 21.5 pounds at 3.5 bars of pressure. As it happened, the air-fuel mixture on the dyno was exactly to BMW specification, so no injector upgrades are needed at this level.

The S52 cams were installed in addition to the previous upgrades, and the VANOS rebuild was

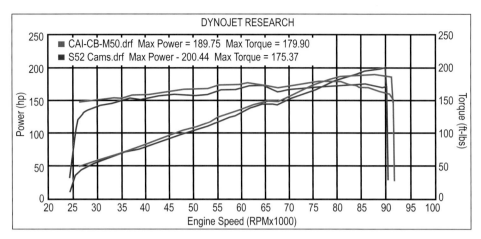

Here are the results of the S52 cam swap. I made 10 more horsepower at the top end but gave up a little torque. However, I did reach my goal of 200 hp at the wheels.

in fourth gear. Torque also remained higher at top RPM with the new cams. Yet both torque and horsepower suffered throughout the normal operating range of the engine.

It is likely that these results show that the limit of development with stock DME tuning has been reached. To take full advantage of these cams requires custom DME tuning.

performed at the same time. This modification finally pushed the project 328i to 200 rear wheel horsepower, boosting peak power by another 10 hp over the previous results using the cold-air intake, cat-back exhaust, and M50 intake manifold. Yet that result is not as impressive as it sounds. The peak horsepower was attained beyond 5,500 rpm and about 82 mph

Cylinder Heads

Cylinder heads are among the easiest parts to work with because there's just not that much difference between them. All E36 heads are dual overhead cam designs, with four valves per cylinder, two each of intake and exhaust.

The M50 and S50 engines use the same cylinder head, and the M52 and S52 engines also share a cylinder head. All the heads used with the E36 are made from aluminum alloy and all flow well enough that there is not a large amount of power to be gained from porting and polishing or other expensive manipulations of the cylinder head.

It is worth noting that while the heads are the same, the S50 and S52 engines use more powerful valvesprings for higher performance.

A Word about Valves

The intake valve is the last part of the engine that the air and gasoline pass on the way into the combustion chamber. The exhaust valve is the

first mechanical part of the engine that the exhaust gas passes on its way out of the car. These are important elements in the power equation because they are usually the tightest points in the flow.

All E36s use a four-valve-per-cylinder design. This means two intake valves and two exhaust valves to feed and exhaust each piston. Valves are moving parts, and they can wear out, break, bend, and burn. A four-valve engine has an advantage. With everything else being equal, two smaller valves can flow more gas than one larger valve. This is because you can generally get more circumferential area out of two smaller valves. Ergo, better flow.

But because you already have four valves in your BMW, what can you do to improve valve flow? If you are building a modified engine, you can source larger valves (within the limits of the head) and valves that are "cut" or "ground" in different ways. Some of those ways flow better than others. If you're having a custom engine built, talk to the engine builder. The

This is what happens when valve timing is off and a valve repeatedly hits the face of a piston. And the result is catastrophic engine failure.

right grind for your application varies based on many other factors, but it's always good to ask the question.

Engine Blocks

Engine blocks are more complicated than cylinder heads in the E36 line, but still easy enough to follow. M50 engine blocks were available in 2.5-liter configurations in North America (and 2.0-liter elsewhere in the world), and the M52 engine was

Secure the E36 Oil Pump

As E36 engines age, longer term and higher mileage problems and failures are becoming more common. One of these issues is that the E36 engine series uses a chain-drive to run its oil pump, and the nut that holds the sprocket onto the oil pump may come loose over time.

The oil pump sprocket nut is left-handed or reverse-threaded, meaning you turn it counterclockwise to tighten. This kind of nut is used when the predominant force applied to a rotating fitting tends to loosen a right-handed nut. However, this nut sometimes comes loose and falls off into the oil pan. When this happens, the oil pump does not turn and engine oil pressure immediately drops to zero. If you don't catch that within a few seconds, the engine is likely to suffer catastrophic damage.

You need to remove the oil pan to access to the oil pump nut and make the proper repair. To remove the oil pan with

the engine still in the car, you need to disconnect the entire front suspension, the front crossmember (also known as the axle support bar), and the steering rack. So this is not a small job at the best of times.

Once the pan is off, you have several options for securing the nut. You can use Loctite red permanent thread sealer. You can try marring the threads of the nut and sprocket shaft with a chisel, or some owners have even tack-welded the nut to the sprocket. Another option is an available replacement nut that has been drilled for safety wire. And this is the best choice. This replacement nut costs about $10. Whatever you choose, the goal is to make certain that the nut is not coming off under any circumstances.

Once the nut is secured, you can reassemble your car. However, ask yourself if this is a good time to check rod bearings or perhaps upgrade the suspension.

available as a 2.5-liter or 2.8-liter model, called the M52B25 and M52B28, respectively.

The corresponding S50 and S52 blocks used in the M3 models were functionally identical to the M50/M52 engine counterparts, but increased bore and stroke to achieve 2,990 cc and 3,201 cc displacement, respectively.

All North American E36-era engine blocks are made of iron, except for the 1997 and 1998 2.8-liter Z3 sports car engines, which were cast from Nikasil aluminum with steel sleeves in the cylinders and weigh 43 pounds less than their iron block counterparts. Some Nikasil aluminum alloy blocks can be sourced in the United States.

Tip: BMW engines are known to suffer from oil starvation in hard cornering, especially on racetracks. If you have the oil pan off the engine for any reason, consider purchasing and installing an oil baffle kit from an aftermarket manufacturer. This is

money well-spent for any performance E36.

Bottom-End Work: Crank, Rods and Pistons

For most street performance E36 builds, you should never have to touch the bottom end of the engine, except for a rebuild due to mileage or damage. Even then rebuilding to stock specifications is probably the best idea unless you're putting on

This rod and piston from the author's Hall of Shame shows what happens when the big end (at the crankshaft) of a connecting rod lets go at speed. A chunk of engine block was knocked loose as the missing part of the rod made its exit from the engine.

A washer fell down an intake port and did this damage to this piston. An entire engine overhaul had to be performed because of a two-cent washer that went missing.

Here's what happens when you have a lean condition or too much spark advance. The fuel detonates and first it ravages the piston face, then eventually blows a hole right through the piston.

Engine Specs

This table shows the bottom-end specification differences for engines commonly sold in E36 cars in North America.

Engine	Bore (mm)	Stroke (mm)	Compression	Displacement (cc)
M50	84.0	75.0	10.0:1	2,494
M50TU	84.0	75.0	10.5:1	2,494
M52B25	84.0	75.0	10.5:1	2,494
M52B28	84.0	84.0	10.2:1	2,793
S50	86.0	85.8	10.5:1	2,990
S52	86.4	89.6	10.5:1	3,152

forced induction to take the engine over 400 hp. At that point, you should look at bottom-end work to reduce the base compression ratio to better accommodate high levels of boost.

To prepare the engine for high-horsepower output, bottom-end work is crucial, as well as perfecting the crank, upgrading to more sturdy connecting rods, and selecting the right reduced compression pistons for use with high boost pressures.

Profile: Dragan's Turbocharged 1998 328i

Dragan Agatonovic has built a 328i, and it may be the ultimate turbocharged E36 application. The research, experimentation, and results he has achieved (and paid for) are instructive to anyone considering a forced induction upgrade to an E36 engine.

This car started out as a 1998 328i sedan, and for the first set of upgrades, Dragan sourced the parts and converted the car to E36 M3 specifications. Then he added an Active Autowerke supercharger kit, but soon decided to switch to turbocharging for his boost.

"I tried drag racing it when I had the supercharger on it, but it would just snap axles. It used to have 328 axles, so I

went with M3 parts because the CV joints are bigger. Then I had a turbo kit with Haltech, but I couldn't get that to run, so I went with the M3 engine with a big Garrett GT35R turbo. But I kept blowing through motors," Dragan says.

The S52 engine has an 87-mm bore making the cylinder walls too thin for the kind of boost levels he wanted. Dragan contacted Evosport and started working with them on a new idea: using the smaller displacement 2.8-liter M52 block with rods and pistons designed for use with a high-boost turbo such as the Garrett. That's the setup he has today.

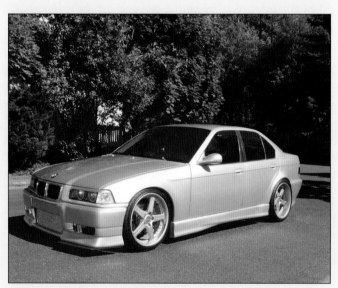

Dragan Agatonovic's 328i project car has gone far beyond the basic build, and Dragan has spared no expense to make this car the ultimate E36.

You can see the right-side inner headlight has been removed to provide a direct air duct to the turbo inlet on this E36. Also notice the front-mounted intercooler in the bottom center.

Profile: Dragan's Turbocharged 1998 328i *CONTINUED*

The empty headlight leads to a tube that directs air to the turbo.

Another look at the headlight turbo inlet. This is a standard upgrade for turbocharged cars. The turbo is located on the right side of the car because of its proximity to the exhaust header.

The air enters here for the turbo, but then it travels down to the intercooler and then up on the intake side, so the whole system flows very well. Note the mesh to keep out all but the smallest particles.

Dragan has another piece of mesh protecting the actual turbo inlet on this Garrett GT35R unit.

"Anything above 20 pounds of boost starts lifting the head. So I went back to a 2.8 block. The machine shop bored out the cylinders just to 84.5 mm and put in extra-large studs and O-rings on the block to keep the engine together. It's currently running a basic pump gas tune at 16 psi of boost, making about 500 wheel horsepower and 500 ft-lbs of torque," Dragan says.

In the end, Dragan went through a tremendous development cycle to bring this car to reliable high performance, with the potential for even more.

"I spent way too much money. I've probably put $100,000 into it with as many engines as I've gone through. Once you go so far above and beyond, it's just the nature of the beast that things are going to break. That was the problem; I had to work through all the bugs. So far, I'm happy with it. It's a freeway monster," he says.

Profile: Dragan's Turbocharged 1998 328i *CONTINUED*

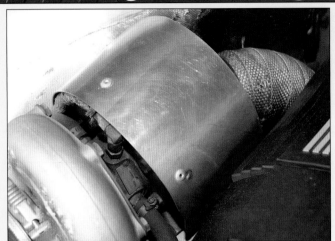

The turbine side of a turbo can become hot enough to glow, so Dragan fabricated this piece of heat shielding to keep that heat away from other components. Also note the exhaust heat wrap on the down-pipe.

This device injects water and methanol into the engine under high boost. This additional material helps cool the cylinders and prevents detonation. It may sound odd, but it works.

Body and Chassis
- Custom Rieger Infinity wide body kit
- E36 M3 complete front and rear subframes, trailing arms, axles, brakes, control arms
- UUC bushings, UUC subframe reinforcement plates, trailing arm reinforcement mounts
- ZKW European glass headlights with 6000k HIDs
- LED turn signals
- Custom 4-inch-high beam engine air intake

Suspension
- Bilstein PSS9 coil-overs
- Racing Dynamics front and rear sway bars
- Racing Dynamics strut bars
- Ground Control adjustable camber plates

Wheels
- Maya RT5 19 x 10 rear and 19 x 9 front

Engine
- M52 block bored to 84.5 mm and O-ringed

- 12-mm head studs with thread inserts and dual pins
- S52 head with dual Ferrea valvesprings
- Evosport custom turbo rods and pistons
- Top mount Garrett GT35R Turbo (.82 A/R)
- Electromotive Tec-3R standalone engine management (PNP by Sias Tuning)
- Cooling mist water methanol injection kit
- UUC Clutch
- Custom 3-inch exhaust with an electric 3-inch cutout

Drivetrain
- M3 ZF5 transmission
- Diffsonline 2.93 rear differential 3-clutch pack 90/30 ramped setup
- M3 CV joints and axles

Interior
- Innovate motorsports air/fuel gauge
- Defi BF Series turbo gauge, fuel pressure gauge, oil temp gauge, water temp gauge
- Apexi AVC-R boost controller ■

IMPROVING HANDLING

Your BMW E36 is one of the best-handling family sedans ever offered to the motoring public. As a premium European sport sedan, BMW prides itself on achieving a smooth ride with excellent grip and predictable handling characteristics. Primarily because of its handling, the E36 is a favorite of autocrossers, track-day enthusiasts, and amateur racers. Many cars offer the same or better power-to-weight ratio, but where BMW really shines is in its handling.

Models such as the 318i and base 325, 328, and 323 cars do not put out big horsepower and torque numbers without extensive modification. But even in stock trim, they have an impressive competition history and are a favorite of performance enthusiasts for their handling. Before you even begin to think about modifying the suspension, you already have a great handling car.

Tip: A lower-powered car can build and maintain speed if it han-

dles well, but a poor-handling car has to slow for every corner.

But that doesn't mean you can't improve things. Every production car is a product of many compromises. A smooth ride versus stiffer shocks and springs, or the tendency to understeer rather than oversteer, for safety. The geometry designed into the stock suspension can be changed, and you can tighten your E36 to race car specs, or just cinch a

Here is the stock stance and wheels of the project 328i when I started. Just the plain dowdy 15-inch wheels and suspension that the factory decided was a good compromise. And all of it is 18 years and 112,000 miles old.

In the world of performance cars, handling often takes a back seat to engine power, but BMW enthusiasts know that there's much more to getting around a curve quickly than stepping on the gas. A good tight suspension and proper alignment with adjustable components transforms your car.

Here's the stance after I replaced the suspension with good quality aftermarket components and a set of 17-inch wheels. The car sits lower, but not too low, and the wheels fill the available space nicely.

few loose places and enjoy a firm and responsive street car.

Tip: If you are interested in learning more about suspension design and development, several good books on the market go into far greater detail about the science that governs suspension work. Carroll Smith's *Tune to Win* and Fred Puhn's classic, *How to Make Your Car Handle,* are great resources.

Warning: Automotive suspensions use tremendously powerful springs that are held under compression when normally installed. Do not attempt to release any automotive spring without the proper tools and instructions or you could seriously injure yourself or even be killed. It costs just a few dollars to have a professional shop install springs, and it is money well spent if you don't have the right tools to do it safely.

Suspension Terms and Concepts

A well-adjusted suspension is critical to creating a good-handling car, yet many of the concepts and relationships behind suspension design and setup are not well-understood.

So what follows is a short description of several basic suspension concepts and how they affect your E36 BMW's handling.

Camber

Camber is defined by how far off of vertical a wheel is when it sits at rest on a flat piece of ground. If you take a small weight on the end of a string and hang it next to the wheel, the angle between the string and the plane of the wheel and tire is the camber angle. If the wheel angles away from the string at the top, that's negative camber. If the wheel angles away from the string at the bottom, that's positive cambers. If the wheel and string are exactly parallel, that's zero camber.

As a rule, performance cars like a bit of negative camber because when the vehicle is cornering, the tires deflect a little bit and negative camber helps keep the largest

---

Camber Plates

The best way to achieve adjustable camber in the front suspension of your E36 is through the use of camber plates. These devices either replace the stock strut tops or fit between the stock strut tops and the strut towers. Most offer camber adjustability by sliding in toward the center of the car a little bit. Some also offer caster adjustment by sliding toward the rear of the car.

Turner Motorsports sells a set of quality camber plates that are not adjustable. These plates are easy to install because they fit between the stock strut top and the strut tower, so you don't even have to disassemble the struts. The plates give you a standard 2 degrees of additional negative camber, but they also raise ride height by about 1/4 inch. For most street applications, this is a great solution.

You can also obtain street-style camber plates made by K-Mac in Australia and Vorshlag or Ground Control Suspension Systems in the United States. Several online retailers sell plates made by these manufacturers. A fully adjustable plate is a more comprehensive upgrade (and more expensive) that replaces the stock strut tops with a fully camber- and caster-adjustable unit. K-Mac, Vorshlag, and Ground Control also make full-race camber plates with metal bushings, but these are not recommended for street use due to increased noise, vibration, and harshness (NVH).

Tip: Remember, you can also buy rear shock tops with firmer bushings to tighten the rear end.

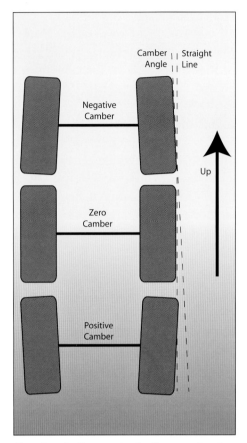

Camber is the easiest alignment set-ting to see. Just look at whether the tops of the tires seem to angle inward or outward.

Caster greatly affects how the E36 steers. Aftermarket caster bushings are a great low-cost investment for these cars.

possible contact patch working for you. It's very possible to go too far with negative camber, however.

E36 suspensions move toward negative camber on the outside wheels as the body rolls while cornering. The E36 uses a MacPherson strut front suspension. The front end gains a small amount of negative camber as it compresses. However, once the control arm crosses past parallel with the ground it begins to move back toward positive camber. The rear suspension is a trailing arm style, with upper and lower control arms. The rear gains significant negative camber as it compresses. All four wheels on your E36 can and should be adjusted for camber.

Tip: Replacing the stock springs with lowering springs without camber plates or some method to adjust the camber in the front creates increased understeer, as the rear end gains substantial camber while the front end camber does not change much.

Caster

Caster is defined as the number of degrees off vertical of the line of the steering axis of the car. That's kind of hard to picture, so consider a straight line drawn from the upper ball joint through the lower ball joint and down to the floor. The lower ball joint tends to be in front of the upper, and the wheel turns

on that line. Caster helps the steering wheel return to straight after cornering because the rolling wheel wants to follow its steering axis. Caster enhances stability and helps the car track in a straight line. You can improve the caster by a couple of degrees on an E36 with a simple bushing change at the back of the lower front control arms.

As with camber, it's possible to have too much caster, and this makes the car hesitant to turn into corners. It's also true that caster turns into camber as the front wheels turn, so it's important not to go too far with adjustments.

In the recommended camber settings later in the chapter, the effect of stock caster has already been integrated, but if you start playing with caster, you need to understand that you're also dialing in more camber when turning.

Toe

Toe is defined as how far off parallel the tires are when they are at rest. If the front ends of the tires are closer together than the rear ends, it's called toe-in. If the rear ends of the tires are closer together, it's toe-out. If the wheels are exactly parallel, it's zero toe.

Toe-in means that both tires are trying to drive toward the centerline of the car, which gives a feeling of stability, but in cornering, you have to turn the steering wheel farther to have both front wheels pointed into the corner. Toe-out means that both wheels are driving away from the centerline of the car, and that creates a wandering feeling, but the car is more eager to turn into a curve. Zero toe is best for straight line speed, because you are not scrubbing the tires at all to go in a straight line.

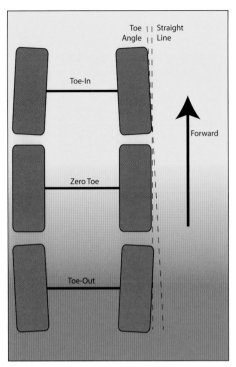

With too much toe-in, the car is constantly scrubbing speed as you drive down the road. That hurts performance and fuel economy, and it makes the car less eager to turn.

As a rule, you want a little bit of toe-in (about 1/16 inch) on the front wheels of a street car, and maybe a little less than that (1/32 or so) of toe-in on the rear wheels. Race cars move toward zero toe and autocrossers sometimes like a bit of toe-out.

One thing to remember is that the steering arm angle changes when you change the ride height of your car. This affects the toe angle, because the outer end of the steering arm makes an arc as the car rises or compresses on its suspension. Ideally, you want to keep the steering arms level with the ground at all times. Caster and camber settings also affect toe, so always set up the toe last of all.

Bump Steer

Bump steer is defined as the change in a tire's steering (mostly

toe) that happens as the tire moves up and down between full extension and full compression. Because the steering arm is fixed at the inboard end and moves up and down at the outboard end, some bump steer is inevitable. You can minimize this by keeping the steering arms level when the car is at rest. The amount of action on the tire becomes more pronounced as the steering arm moves farther from level, so starting from level is the best you can achieve.

If the front tires are parallel when the car is at rest, and you move one tire to full compression (like driving over a bump), that tire is pulled out of parallel by the movement of the steering arm. You experience this as bump steer, an unplanned change of steering direction due to traveling over the bump.

Bump steer is a function of geometry and in a strut-suspended car like the E36, there is little to no bump steer in the front end regardless of how high or low you run the car, because there is little to no camber change.

E36 Suspension Design

This section describes the basic design of the E36 suspension for the 318i, 325, 328, 323, and M3 models 1992–1999. The 318ti hatchback and the Z3 sports car use a different rear suspension design inherited from the E30 chassis. The BMW E36 suspension is fundamentally the same across the entire product line. Small differences exist in parts from different years and models, but the overall design strategy remains the same. The following is a basic description of the suspension you find under the car.

Front Suspension

An E36 front suspension is relatively simple in design. On each side of the car there is an L-shaped lower control arm attached to the chassis in two places. The part is sometimes called an "A-arm" or "wishbone" for historical reasons. On some cars they are actually shaped like a capital *A* or a wishbone. The lower control arm is made from thick forged steel, and it supports the hub and bearing carrier upright assembly on a ball joint.

Redesigned aftermarket control arms are not readily available because there has been no need for such a part. However, consider that the late E30 M3 front lower control arms were made from aluminum and fit the E36. These lightweight units make a nice upgrade if you're going all-out with your car. The aftermarket manufacturer Meyle has also produced a line of E36 front control arms with upgraded ball joints, and these are a good choice for a performance build.

The upright assembly includes a spindle for the bearing and hub, a flange to attach the steering arm, a flange on which to attach the brake caliper, and a flange on the back to attach the strut assembly. The MacPherson Strut assembly bolts to the backside of the upright assembly with two lower bolts and to the flange for strength. The strut includes a spring perch and support structure, a spring, a shock absorber, and a top mount that bolts into the strut tower built into the chassis of the car. A U-shaped anti-sway bar is attached to the chassis in two places, and on non-M cars, attached to the two lower control arms with drop links. The M3 connects the sway bar drop link to the strut itself.

On an E36 with the stock front suspension, caster is set for you with

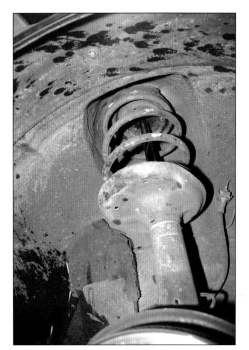

Here is the stock strut on the project 328i. Age and mileage has taken a toll.

The stock rear spring and shock are pretty tired and need to be replaced no matter what.

the angles of the strut and the lower control arm. The stock strut top (also called a "hat") is fixed, and does not allow for camber changes. Yet the entire assembly is held in place with soft rubber bushings that allow quite a bit of flex. But that's why there's an aftermarket, to provide firm bushings and adjustable components. The best way to adjust caster is by using firm offset bushings at the rear mount of the lower control arm. See the Stage 1 suspension upgrade project for a procedure to install these.

Rear Suspension

The rear suspension is substantially different, in that the shock absorber does not ride within the spring. On each side of the rear of the car, an upper control arm supports the spring in a perch. At its outer end, the upper control arm connects to the top of the rear bearing carrier upright assembly. The axle half-shafts come from the dif-

ferential and final drive assembly at the centerline of the car and pass through the bearing carrier to drive the rear hubs. The rear disc brakes are also mounted on the rear uprights. A flange on the backside of the upright toward the rear of the car provides a mount for the rear shock absorber.

A stamped-steel trailing arm mounts forward of the rear wheel wells and attaches to the front ends of the rear uprights. Each side also has a stamped-steel lateral control arm that attaches to the chassis inboard of the hub assembly, and these attach to the bottom of the rear hub assembly. These control arms limit the lateral movement of the rear wheels, while the trailing arms limit fore and aft motion.

The rear anti-sway bar is attached to the chassis in two places toward the center of the car and uses drop links to attach to the upper control arm on either side of the car.

The stock rear suspension allows some adjustment with eccentric bolts, but the system is put together using soft rubber bushings. You can tighten the suspension quite a lot with just a little effort and expense by using aftermarket adjustable lower control arms and upgraded polyurethane or other

firm bushings throughout the system. Be wary of dialing in too much camber in the rear. You want only about –1.5 degrees on each side or you start to increase understeer in corners.

Wheel Alignment

Just as all the great engine parts in the world won't help you much if they aren't properly tuned, the suspension needs to be tuned to give you the performance you've paid for. Suspension tuning is every bit as important as engine tuning, and in some respects it's harder to do. Tuning an engine, you can use a dyno and ECU readouts to measure torque, horsepower, timing, and air/fuel ratio. With suspension tuning, you have to rely more on feel and personal preference. You can (and you should) use accurate tools to set up the suspension, but it's harder to identify the optimum setup.

One skill that professional racing drivers cultivate is the ability to describe a car's handling characteristics in precise terms, and to repeat a test lap the same way every time for a valid test of new suspension settings. The rest of us just have to work at it as best we can.

Tip: The factory alignment settings are very good for most street driving. These settings are optimized to minimize NVH and maximize the fuel economy and tire wear. If you don't need a different alignment for track or autocross competition, it's best to leave things more or less in the stock configuration.

Start by having your car aligned to the factory specifications. If you have substantial aftermarket modifications such as caster/camber plates, adjustable shock absorbers, or a coil-over suspension, you have more adjustability than with the stock components. Then, working from stock, make incremental changes and test the results until the car feels good to you. Don't be afraid to keep adjusting until the car no longer feels good, then work your way back to the optimum setting.

Aligning Your Car

For most street performance applications, it is best to have your car aligned professionally. Choose the alignment shop carefully, because the low-end shops do not employ technicians with the experience to align your car to custom settings. They can only set it to factory specifications. Find a shop that is experienced with custom and performance alignment.

That being said, for street use you aren't generally too far off the stock alignment settings. Things change when you go autocrossing because autocrossers often prefer a setup that induces more oversteer than you want for street use. Therefore, autocrossers frequently learn to align their cars themselves, so they can change their setup when they arrive at an event, and change it back before heading home.

Changing your own front camber is easiest with a set of adjustable camber plate strut tops, but with a camber gauge you can change this setting in moments. Rear camber is slightly adjustable with the stock lower camber arms, but if you plan to adjust on the fly or you want more camber than the stock arms allow, you want to invest in a set of adjustable lower camber arms in the rear. Setting the rear camber still requires that camber gauge.

Caster is more difficult to set unless the strut tops have that adjustment built in. Without those tops, caster changes require replacing bushings under the car.

The main setting you can change yourself easily is toe. The BMW suspension design allows you to set both front and rear toe.

Making Toe Plates

Two classic methods are used for setting toe. The first is to use a set of toe plates. These are just flat rectangular plates that are about as wide as the tires, and tall enough to sit snugly against the tires. Roughly speaking, you want the toe plates to cover the lower half of the tires.

First, decide which long edge of the toe plate is the bottom and mark it. Then cut a small slot about 1-inch long 3-inches up from the bottom on each short edge of the plate. That's where the measuring tape goes. The two toe plates should be identical.

To use the toe plates, you need two identical tape measures with the little hooks on the ends of the tapes. Have a friend to help you, and stand each toe plate snugly against the tires with the bottom ends on the floor. Then hook the two tape measures into the little slots in front of and in back of the tires. Pull the tapes

tight and pass the tapes through the slots on the toe plate on the other side. You can now read the distance between the toe plates in front of and in back of the tires. The difference in distance is the toe reading.

Obviously or maybe not obviously if the toe plates are much wider than the tire diameter, the readings are exaggerated. You want to take the readings as close to the tire diameter as possible. What you're looking for is the difference, which will be between 1/16 inch and perhaps 3/16 inch. For example, if the forward tape reads 80 inches and the rearward tape reads 80 1/16 inch, you have 1/16 inch of toe-in. If the readings are identical, you have zero toe. If the front measurement is longer than the rear, you have toe-out.

Stringing a Car

Stringing a car is a more comprehensive procedure, and it's also more time consuming and harder to do. First you find the car's centerline by measuring from some fixed point, usually the inboard mounts for the lower control arms, front and rear.

Then you use four heavy objects (jack stands work well) and lengths of string to create two parallel lines on either side of the car, equidistant from the car's measured centerline. Make sure the lines are at least as long as the car. Now you can measure the distance between the string line and any point on the car. This is often used to detect prior crash damage. You can see if the car's chassis has been bent because the same fixed points on either side of the car are different distances from the parallel strings.

For alignment purposes, make sure that the front wheels are totally straight with respect to the chassis.

Then you can measure from the string to the front edge of a tire, and to the rear edge and have the toe setting for that tire individually. Repeat the procedure for all four tires and you can find the total toe for front or rear by adding the individual toe readings together. You may find that one wheel is at zero toe with respect to the centerline of the car, while the other has a significant amount of toe. Or both tires may have varying amounts of toe. Once you have the measurements, you can make changes to square up your car and have the alignment you want.

Tip: Use a carpenter's square to be sure you have an exact square measurement to each point.

It is generally faster to use toe plates for a quick alignment adjustment, but the tradeoff is that toe plates can give you only a look at one pair of wheels at a time, and it yields only a total toe measurement. You can see the total toe of the fronts or the rears, but you can't tell if the car is generally straight and the same front to rear. So, to do a full alignment yourself, you want to string the car to see all the relationships between the wheels.

Centering a Steering Wheel

Centering a steering wheel is part of the front wheel alignment process. Most often, different toe settings on the tires (or crash damage) is the reason the steering wheel does not sit level when you're traveling straight ahead. To level the wheel, you need to make opposite and equal changes to each of the front wheel toe settings. By lengthening one steering rod and shortening the other, while keeping the wheels pointed straight ahead, the steering wheel rotates and you can true it up.

Some Basic Alignment Settings

As a rule, when you're doing your own alignment, you tend to measure in inches, because you're working with measuring tapes. Yet most repair manuals express alignment settings in degrees, because they assume an alignment shop with modern alignment equipment will be doing the work.

E36 Suspension Modification Stages

Perhaps the most important performance enhancements you can make are to your car's suspension. Even drag racers carefully consider their cars' suspension because fore-and-aft weight transfer under acceleration can be optimized. Obviously, suspension is critical for track-day or autocross use, but any street car benefits from a fresh, firm suspension. Even if you're building a show car where the stance is the primary consideration, you can still make the car enjoyable to drive with a few smart mods to the suspension.

With an understanding of the basic stock suspension on the E36, you can plan the suspension improvements that work for you. There are a number of factors to consider that relate mainly to accumulated mileage and the way you plan to use your car. A dedicated track day or racing car may be far more intensely modified than your daily driver. Be aware that most of the handling improvement comes in the basic Stage 1 upgrades that can be applied to any car. For most of us, that's where the sweet spot between performance and comfort is found.

It is important to note that for any E36, the suspension shows significant wear by about 60,000 miles

E36 Alignment Specifications

The table below offers some basic E36 alignment settings that are approximately equal to the stock settings. The actual factory settings vary from year to year and model to model. The settings provided here are approximate for most E36 cars, and if you want stock settings, an alignment shop has them.

	Stock Suspension (degrees)	Sport Suspension (degrees)	M3 (degrees)
Front Total Toe-In	+0.18	+0.18	+0.10
Front Camber	−0.30	−0.50	−0.55
Front Caster	+3.41	+3.50	+6.38
Rear Toe	+0.24	+0.24	+0.30
Rear Camber	−1.40	−2.00	−1.45

The table below shows some alternate settings that are popular with street performance enthusiasts, autocross competitors, and track day enthusiasts.

	Street (degrees)	Autocross (degrees)	Track (degrees)
Total Front Toe	+0.06	-0.06	0.00
Front Camber	−2.00	−3.50	−4.50
Front Caster	+6.00	+6.00	+6.00
Total Rear Toe	+0.10	+0.10	+0.10
Rear Camber	−1.50	−2.50	−2.75

of use, and by 100,000 miles every E36 suspension requires replacing of all consumable components. Because virtually all of the available E36 cars show this mileage in the modern era, you should plan on a complete suspension overhaul as part of your upgrade plan.

Stage 1: Upgrading Front Struts, Rear Shocks, and Springs

As with most systems on a car, you upgrade the suspension in stages. The first stage is simply to install fresh components throughout the suspension, selecting new stock control arms and steering rods with

This rear shock is long dead, but people don't notice rear shocks as much as fronts. So even if some updates have been done on a car, chances are good that the fronts have been done but the rears were ignored.

The old stock strut and the new H&R Touring Cup strut side by side. I re-use the strut top from the stock unit and add an H&R spring to the new setup.

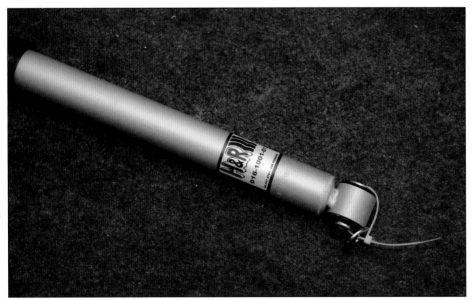

The rear end of an E36 uses a basic steel shock. The H&R Touring Cup kit comes with both front and rear units that are matched to the H&R springs. The H&R kit shocks are not adjustable, but they are matched to the H&R springs for the BMW's weight.

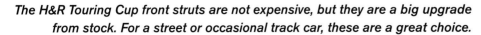

The H&R Touring Cup front struts are not expensive, but they are a big upgrade from stock. For a street or occasional track car, these are a great choice.

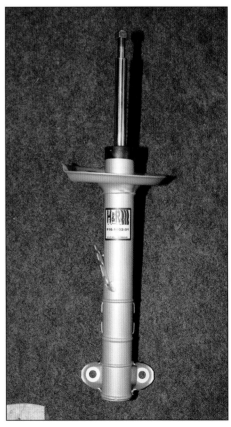

fresh ball joints, but using upgraded polyurethane bushings throughout, non-adjustable performance struts in front, and comparable shock absorbers at the rear. A new set of springs about 1 to 2 inches shorter and up to about 15 percent stiffer than the stock components is a good modification. This alone sharpens the steering and handling on a car that is now at least 16 to 24 years old.

In any modern car, *strut* is used synonymously with *shock* to define a shock absorber because a MacPherson strut and a traditional shock absorber serve the same function, to dampen suspension motion. A strut also serves as the upper control arm and spring perch, which is nice when you make changes to the system. The E36 uses a MacPherson strut on the front suspension and a traditional spring and shock absorber in the rear.

More than anything else, the struts and shocks on your E36 (or any car) keep the wheels in contact with the ground by absorbing the spring recoil when you drive over a bump. Without shocks, the springs can launch the car into the air when they are suddenly compressed by a bump and then release their energy. Shock absorbers earned their name because they "catch" the car when the suspension compresses and make the springs release their energy over time. Moreover, the shocks make the car's ride more comfortable and confident. You should always keep the shocks in good condition.

Tip: A common mistake people make with adjustable shocks is to set them up as stiffly as possible. Stiff shocks feel like high performance because you can feel every bump. You may think you can tell the difference between driving over a dime and a nickel, but that's not necessarily helping keep the tires on the ground. Most adjustable shocks are quite stiff to begin with, so start with them on their softest setting and work your way up through the range. Chances are you'll find that a medium-soft setting gives you the best all-around results, especially if you're using stiffer and lower springs.

A variety of replacement struts and shocks are made to fit your E36. The E36 front strut design allows the amateur mechanic to replace struts with readily available tools. However, if you change the springs at the same time you change the struts, or if you change alignment settings, you should have your car professionally aligned afterward.

Stage 1: Spring Upgrades

At the easy and low-cost end of the suspension upgrade spectrum, you can buy performance spring kits that install into the stock locations. These kits offer pretty good spring rates for most applications. Generally, these springs are 10 to 15 percent stiffer than stock, and drop the ride height anywhere from 1/2 inch to 2 inches. It's a good idea to replace the shock/strut assemblies at the same time as the springs, but it's not necessary if the existing struts are in good shape. The job is easy enough to do so that you can replace the shocks later when needed or affordable.

If you choose springs that are more than about 15 percent stiffer than stock, you need to upgrade the front struts and rear shocks to units that are capable of controlling the greater spring rates you're installing. Remember that a spring rate works both ways: compression and extension. The firmer spring offers more resistance to compression, and then delivers more force to re-extend itself. The dampening ability of stock struts and shocks is overwhelmed. It's counterintuitive, but with stiff springs installed, you actually enjoy a smoother ride with firmer shocks that match the dampening rate to the new spring rate.

The spring rates that feel "comfortable" and give the car some compliance for street driving are going to differ based on the struts you choose. An entry-level Bilstein or Koni shock can only be paired with springs up to 450 pounds in the front and 550 pounds in the rear before it starts to feel extremely choppy. On the other hand, a high-end shock, such as the MCS, can run springs up to 850 pounds in the front and 950 pounds in the rear and still feel very streetable.

H&R gives you an attractive set of blue springs with the Touring Cup kit. These springs are about 10 percent stiffer than new stock springs and offer a significant upgrade from the OEM products without making the ride too rough.

As a general baseline, I recommend the following spring rates:

Street	450 front/550 rear
Autocross	550 front/650 rear
Track	750 front/850 rear
Race	850 front/950 rear

For an inverted rear coil-over shock absorber style, such as those found on high-end double, triple, and quad-adjustable shocks, I recommend a 900-pound front/400-pound rear or 1,000-pound front/500-pound rear spring rate. The drastic rear rate change is due to the spring being moved more outboard than the stock location, which changes its motion ratio from about 0.44 to 0.88:1. The decrease in leverage applied to the spring is the reason for the lower spring rate.

Stage 2: Adjustable Front Struts and Rear Lateral Control Arms

The second stage of upgrades involves purchasing adjustable struts all around and replacing the front strut tops with camber-adjustable units. Rear suspension modifications in the second stage also include adjustable rear lower lateral control arms for camber adjustment.

When experts talk about shock absorbers of any kind, they use the terms "bump" or "compression" and "rebound" to describe compression and extension resistance, respectively. All struts resist both bump and rebound, but they may not resist both motions equally. If you have adjustable struts, you can set the resistance level to harder or softer settings, but sometimes only in the rebound direction. If you have purchased double-adjustable struts, you can set bump and rebound resistance separately.

The serious track enthusiast should replace the stock strut tops with an adjustable unit like this. This gives you more camber, more caster, and the ability to adjust the strut's resistance.

This is the top of a remote reservoir shock with an adjustable top mount, reinforced strut tower, and separate adjustments. Compression resistance is adjusted by the dial on the left, while rebound resistance is adjusted at the top of the strut rod.

The most popular brands of aftermarket struts to consider include H&R, Bilstein, and Koni. All of these are good products, and each has its own fierce devotees. The differences from brand to brand are not as pronounced as the differences between different strut styles within each brand.

For example, among non-adjustable replacement sport strut units, H&R, Koni, and Bilstein are by far the most popular brands. Bilstein does a lot of OEM work for automakers, and their reputation is solid. H&R also makes a great strut, and it's the brand I chose for the project E36.

In each of those brands, you can also upgrade to single- and double-adjustable coil-over struts. As you move up the feature and adjustability ladder, the prices become higher, but you can then set the car up easily for a track day, and then dial it back for comfortable street use. You can purchase a set of stock replacements for about $1,000, or move up to basic coil-overs for just a few hundred dollars more.

At the high end of performance parts, you find advanced products from KW, Motion Control, Ohlins, and Moton. Some of these are four-way adjustable with low-speed and high-speed compression and rebound settings. The high-end products from these manufacturers are far more expensive than any other options (well over $10,000 for a set), and so they are generally limited to race or track cars because of the expense. However, they can also be adjusted to ride well on the street. KW and Motion Control also make more affordable units.

Tip: After installing sport suspension, many drivers complain that their cars ride too stiffly. So they soften the shocks, but the problem only becomes worse. This is because the dampening rate of the struts must be matched to the rate of the new springs. If this is happening to you, try stiffening the shocks until they can adequately control the springs.

In the rear, the lateral control arms hold the lower end of the hub, and you can make some camber adjustment by purchasing adjustable control arms. I install a set of these later in the chapter. The factory control arms are slightly adjustable for increased rear camber, but are made from comparatively weak mild steel stampings. Aftermarket lower control arms are machined from aluminum and offer a threaded end for adjustment, and they come with your choice of rubber or poly bushings or with rod ends for maximum precision and control.

You can purchase adjustable rear lateral control arms from many manufacturers, and all of them are better than the stock stamped units. All online E36 parts retailers offer some easily adjustable complete replacement control arms, and they also have stock-type units that are reinforced. You can choose from Turner, Megan Racing, Vivid Racing, and more. Because these are such simple parts to make, retailers tend to carry their own branded parts; they are all pretty similar. I chose the Turner Motorsports units because of their high-quality and lightweight aluminum construction and ease of adjustment.

Stage 3: Coil-Over Suspension Upgrade

At the top of the suspension hierarchy, you can buy coil-over suspension kits. In the front, these kits replace the stock strut body with a threaded-body unit of a specific diameter and/or design that accepts springs of a specific coil diameter. Large adjustment nuts move up and down the outside of the threaded bodies to allow you to assemble and disassemble the unit without a spring compressor.

A true coil-over conversion for the rear of the E36 is quite easy and can be achieved with some simple reinforcement of the rear upper mount area and an appropriate shock product. For track or autocross cars, this modification is highly recommended and offers a myriad of advantages; the only tradeoff is cost.

You can purchase rear aftermarket coil-over spring perches, but there are specific geometry challenges with these products. The rear upper control arm moves in an arc, but a coil-over spring is straight. Standard ride height adjusters either unload at full droop and create a noise as they reseat, or they bow the spring sideways, creating non-linear spring response. This tendency can be

For the racer or serious track enthusiast, you'll be looking at a full coil-over setup like this Koni. Coil-overs give you the most adjustment of any suspension option.

An adjustable rear lower control arm (or camber arm) allows you to set rear camber beyond the range of the stock unit. I have a procedure to install these later in the chapter.

properly fixed with a product such as the Ground Control articulating spring perches. A set of these costs about $230, and they are well worth the expense.

One big reason that track day and autocross enthusiasts prefer coil-overs is that ride height can be set individually per wheel. This allows you to adjust corner weights and spring preload. Because you can remove and install springs on your own, a set of coil-overs offers the possibility of multiple sets of springs of varying rates for your different driving events.

Several aftermarket retailers offer coil-over kits for the E36, including a set of springs chosen for the car's weight. Many coil-over kits include separate adjustment nuts that let you set the total height of the assembly as well as the compression on the spring. This allows you to set ride height and retain the full travel of the suspension while separately adjusting the spring preload. Other high-end kits are engineered for maximum stroke. Having separate shock body length and spring preload adjustments reduces suspension stroke and overall shock oil volume.

Every modification comes with tradeoffs, and the first thing to know is that good coil-over kits are extremely expensive, two to three times the price of a good set of performance shocks and springs, and ranging up to $13,000 or more. But an inexpensive set of coil-overs is no bargain. Many cheap coil-overs are too stiff and ruin the car's ride quality. Conversely, a good set of coil-overs ride just as well, if not better, than stock and handle better, even with spring rates that are 400 percent of stock. A set of JRZ RS, Ohlins, DFV, or MCS

SA dampeners ride very well on the street as well as on the track. These are expensive modifications, yet still the most highly recommended suspension for any discerning street driver who wants the ultimate in handling and comfort.

All high-end shocks, such as those mentioned above, are going to be fantastic on the street. Even using high spring rates, these products can handle any track and autocross use you want. The only real drawback from a high-end dampener is the extremely high purchase price. An entry-level MCS single-adjustable shock with all the additional parts needed to install it (including camber plates, upper strut mounts, coil-over springs, tender springs, and so on) can run as much as $4,000 (not including installation and setup labor). Stepping up to double- or triple-adjustable shocks sends the price well above $10,000.

Stage 3: Measuring Ride Height

If you have upgraded to a coil-over suspension, some new adjustments are available to you. Because you can change springs easily and set the total strut height and spring compression individually, you have more control over the ride height and the weight distribution to the four corners of the vehicle.

To begin, let's look at the stock ride height that BMW specified for the E36. For manufacturer's purposes, ride height is always measured from the center of the wheel arch (assuming you have stock bodywork) to the bottom center of the wheel lip. This technique eliminates tire sidewall height differences from the measurement.

Stock ride height is important to know because most project cars

have substantial mileage, and all springs sag over time. So if you plan to purchase sport springs that offer a 1.5-inch drop, be aware that the promised drop is relative to the factory specifications, and your particular car may already be riding lower than the official height. The tire sidewall height also affects perceived ride height.

On E36 cars equipped with 15-inch wheels, BMW specifies a ride height of about 20 inches, while 16-inch wheels should produce a ride height of roughly 20.5 inches and 17-inch wheels should result in a ride height around 21 inches. Small differences exist between models and year-to-year, but these numbers are a good baseline.

Stage 3: Setting Ride Height and Corner Weights with Coil-Overs

First, park on a flat, level surface. Set the basic ride height to approximate levels for your purposes. Measure the ride height from the bottom of the rim to the top of the wheel arch on each corner of the car and adjust each corner until ride height is where you want it. When you have the ride height set, you can make adjustments to set the corner weights and correct the alignment. Then, go back and check it all again because each change you make affects the others. Don't forget to check and see what your changes have done to the angle of the lower control arm and the steering arms!

You need a set of wheel scales to set weights. Sometimes scales can be rented from racing shops, but a better plan is to find a tuner or racing shop with a set of scales and take your car there for corner weighting. It takes a lot less time and effort, and probably yields better results. Be sure to bring your car in its usual configuration and sit in the driver's seat while the weights are taken. By adjusting each strut's total length and spring compression up or down a little, you can maintain a level ride (or the angle you want) and equalize diagonal weights and ride height side-to-side in the car.

E36 models generally handle best with a half-inch rake front to rear as measured from the pinch welds. The wheel arches are larger on the front to accommodate the steering action of the wheel, so having a half-inch rake front to rear via the wheel arches result in a car that sits substantially higher in the rear.

Project: Front Suspension Upgrade

One of the most common handling projects that owners can undertake themselves is to upgrade the stock struts and springs with aftermarket products that offer increased performance and also lower the car. Lowering the car looks great and helps the handling because it lowers the car's center of gravity and roll center.

This project installs the H&R Touring Cup kit of struts and springs on the project 328i, but the instructions work for all E36 models. The springs are designed to lower the car about 1.5 inches, and the struts offer more resistance appropriate to the new spring rate. With almost 20 years and 112,000 miles on the stock struts and bushings, the project 328i desperately needed this upgrade. I did not expect the car to actually be lowered as much as the kit indicated, because the stock springs had already sagged quite a bit, especially in the rear.

Tip: BMW enthusiasts frequently shorten the term "Front Control Arm Bushings" to FCAB in written discussions.

For this project I chose a complete kit of struts and springs from H&R and Whiteline poly bushings. In addition, I ordered OEM replacement front lower control arms and both inner and outer steering tie rods. For the bushings, I chose offsets for the rear mounts of the front lower control arms. This modification gives you about 2 to 3 degrees of additional caster on the front wheels. (See the section on offset bushings later in this chapter for more information.)

Here is the parts list:

- OEM bump stops
- OEM front lower control arms
- OEM inner and outer steering rods
- H&R Touring Cup front kit with struts and springs
- Whiteline Front Control Arm Bushing (FCAB)

These special tools and supplies are required for working on the front suspension:

- Ball-joint separator
- Three-jaw hub puller
- Hydraulic press with dies to fit the rear control arm mount bushing
- Anti-seize lubricant

Tip: If you are replacing the FCAB with a new stock bushing, you need the special BMW-specific bushing installer tool.

Follow These Steps

1 Raise the car to a comfortable working height on the lift (or on a set of sturdy jack stands) and remove the front wheels. If you have a jack or shop support, place it under the suspension on the side you're working with. This is to support the suspension when you remove the upper strut mount nuts.

Tip: Put masking tape on the wheel well edges to keep the struts from damaging the paint when pulling them out.

2 Now choose a side, and begin. Because you will be replacing the lower control arms and steering tie rods as well as the struts, you want to remove the front brake caliper and unplug the anti-lock brake sensor at the connection on the wheel well. Support the brake caliper by hanging it from any available strong point, such as the strut spring, with a piece of safety wire to avoid stress on the brake flex line. This allows the front hub assembly to be removed.

You must also unbolt the sway bar drop link from the lower control arm. You can use any kind of wrench you like, but standard combination wrenches work best for this procedure.

Here are the wheel and brake sensor connections after being disconnected at the wheel well.

Here's the box in the wheel well where you disconnect the wheel sensors.

3 Remove the nut holding the lower control arm to the upright, and strike the control arm briskly with a hammer to break the ball joint loose. This may take several vigorous swings. The control arm should come loose from the car at this point. The upright should remain supported by the strut. You can also use a ball joint separator. Avoid using a "pickle fork"–style separator; it can damage the boot on the control arm.

You need to break free the stock ball joint. There's not a lot of room to work there, but be patient and it pops loose.

The new ball joint benefits from some anti-seize to make this job easier the second time.

To refresh the suspension, you need both lower control arms. If you don't replace these, everything else you do won't make much difference.

4 Use the hub puller to remove the rear-mount bushing from the control arm. This will likely destroy the soft rubber stock bushing, leaving the center attached to the old control arm. This is okay. Discard or recycle the old control arm. Move to the hydraulic press and press the metal sleeve of the old bushing out of the rear mount.

Next, press in the new bushing.

If you have purchased an offset bushing to increase caster, orient the new bushing so that the hole in the bushing sits to the outside of the vehicle, nearest to the tab on the bushing carrier.

Tip: Use a center punch to make an indentation in the end of the control arm so the hub puller centers itself when pulling the rear mount bushing off.

This rear control arm bushing is worn out and mushy. It's going to let the lower control arm move all over the place.

Take a center punch and make an indentation in the center of the rod. This allows the puller to center itself and work better.

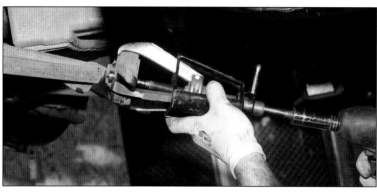

You need to remove the rear bushing with a hub puller. It's on there pretty tight.

With a good coating of anti-seize, place the new offset bushing onto the new lower control arm.

5 Spread a little anti-seize onto the rear end of the new control arm and press the new bushing onto the control arm by hand. You might need to use a light tap or two from the dead-blow hammer to encourage the bushing onto the rod. It does not have to go on all the way just yet.

Install the new control arm and tighten the fasteners at the two forward locations; then locate the rear mount as appropriate. You want to apply upward pressure on the arm to seat the ball joints in the arm snugly. That applies enough friction for you to tighten the new nylon lock nuts. A socket wrench gives you all the torque you need.

If you do not seat the taper of the ball joint well, the ball joint simply spins when you try to tighten the locking nut.

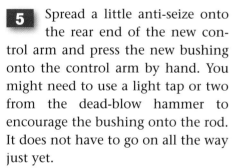

A hydraulic press is the best solution for removing the old bushing and installing the new poly offset bushing.

Install the offset bushing with the hole nearest the mounting tab on each side. If you do it the other way, you eliminate all the caster.

Use a dead blow hammer to tap the bushing onto its rod. Be patient and tap around the perimeter and it goes right on.

Position the control arm and its bushing to the mounting point. You may need to tap the bushing tighter to line it up perfectly.

With the ball joint in place and the rear bushing bolted up, the third point on the lower control arm triangle is the hub assembly. Use anti-seize here, too.

You should always replace the steering boots, as these keep dust and grit out of the steering gear.

6 Remove the nut holding the steering tie rod end to the upright, and use the ball joint separator to break the tie rod free. Replace the tie rod end and the steering rod back to the steering rack. Attach the tie rod to the upright last, and adjust the steering rod length to a reasonable setting. You will be aligning the car at the conclusion of the project, so it just has be close enough to get your car to the alignment shop.

Be sure to replace the zip-ties that hold the dust boot onto the steering rack and tie rod. Also be sure to replace the inner tie rod and its lock plate according to the factory shop manual instructions.

Tip: You can make an inexpensive upgrade by using the 1998 or later M3 strut tops and swapping them left to right. You gain a degree or so of camber and some additional caster with this modification.

The tie rod is attached just behind the brake rotor and should come off easily. It will be replaced, so don't worry too much about its condition.

You can see where the locking tab has been flattened to allow you to unscrew the inner tie rod. Be sure to replace the locking tab and use it to lock the tie rod in place.

New tie rod ends really help the car's steering feel, and give you precise alignment.

7 Now remove the nuts that hold the strut to the strut tower, and then remove the bolts that hold the strut to the upright. The strut tower top nuts can be easily removed with a socket wrench or an open-end wrench. The bolts holding the strut to the upright need a socket wrench, and an air wrench with socket extension often makes this job easier. You can now remove the strut from the car.

You will be reusing the strut top (unless you bought a replacement), but that's the only part going back in the car. Use the strut spring compressor to take the tension off the assembly, then remove the center nut that holds the strut top to the strut and release the spring.

Warning: If you don't have strut spring compressors, do not attempt to do this job! Take the old and new parts to any auto shop, where they have a wall-mounted tool that handles this job safely and easily. It shouldn't cost more than a few dollars to have the pros take care of this for you.

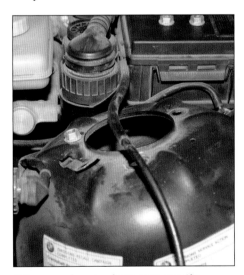

When you're ready to remove the strut, just undo these three nuts and the whole assembly drops right out of the strut tower.

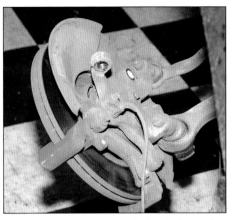

With the strut removed, the hub and brake assembly just hang loose. If you were to undo the lower control arm at the same time, the hub and brake would hang by the brake flex line, so be sure to do these one at a time.

A proper strut compressor at a professional shop makes short work of changing the struts. You can use the small strut compressors that they sell at auto parts stores, but it's cheaper and safer to take the struts to a shop and have them done.

8 Assemble the new strut with the new springs and new OEM bump stop. The top should go on easily with the shorter performance spring, but still likely requires the use of spring compressors or a shop strut tool. When assembled, place the strut into the strut tower and align the studs on the strut top with the holes in the tower and tighten the retaining nuts, then attach the strut to the upright. Camber is set for you with this geometry.

This picture shows the new strut and spring being assembled with the stock strut top.

Installation is just the reverse of removal. You stick the strut up into the tower, line up the studs, and put the nuts on. That's all there is to it.

With the new strut and spring installed, there's a bit of color and a whole lot of performance under the fenders.

At the hub assembly, three connections fix the strut in place as the upper control arm of the suspension.

Warning: Never use air tools to tighten the top nut on the strut assembly. An impact gun can loosen the internal nut that holds the shim stack together, ruining the new strut. Also, never use Vise-Grips or pliers on the strut shaft. You must make absolutely certain that you never scratch the strut shaft for any reason. It is chrome plated and strong, but one tiny nick can ruin the strut!

9 Reassemble the brakes, reconnect the ABS sensors, and mount the wheels. Immediately take your car to a professional alignment shop for a full four-wheel alignment.

Project: Rear Suspension Upgrade

To go along with the front suspension upgrade, here are the instructions for the rear upgrade using the same H&R kit. Note that you can perform either of these projects separately, although it is best to do all four corners at one time.

Tip: BMW enthusiasts frequently shorten the term "Rear Trailing Arm Bushing" to RTAB in written discussions.

This project does not replace the rear trailing arm bushings, which is a critical upgrade procedure for E36 BMWs, so it is documented as a separate project.

Here is a parts list:

- OEM bump stops
- H&R Touring Cup rear kit with shocks and springs
- Special tools and supplies required for front suspension
- Lever to insert the spring

Follow These Steps

1 Raise the car to a comfortable working height on the lift (or on a set of sturdy jack stands) and remove the rear wheels. If you have a jack or shop support, place it under the suspension on the side on which you're working. This is to stop the suspension from springing down when you remove the top nut on the shock.

A shop stand is a good idea when undoing the rear suspension. The spring is exerting a lot of downward force on the control arms.

This is the condition of my 18-year-old rear bump stops on the project 328i, so these are going to be replaced for sure. Do not decide to skip these little parts, as they keep the shocks from being damaged under heavy compression.

2 Go in through the trunk and disconnect the tops of the shocks. You have to remove some trim pieces for access. You see three nuts on studs coming through the shock tower. You need only remove the two nuts on the sides. The central nut goes with the shock. When the tops are free, you can unbolt the bottoms and remove the shocks from the car.

Open the trunk and you find the rear shock tops in their own little strut towers.

On the passenger's side, other parts obscure the rear shock top, but there's enough room to remove the tops.

3 Without the shocks to limit droop, the rear suspension should drop as you lower the jack or support. With the rear suspension completely loose, you should be able to remove the old spring by hand. You may also want to remove the rubber pads that hold the spring and clean those while you have the spring out.

When you let the rear suspension droop, you can insert a big lever into the control arm to bend it down enough to release the rear spring.

4 To replace the new spring, you may need to use a long and heavy pry bar to squeeze the spring slightly and work it into position on the rubber pads. Enlist the help of a friend and be very careful during this procedure. Automotive springs can be dangerous if they slip while compressed. Fortunately, performance springs tend to be a little shorter than new stock springs; these went in with just a little encouragement from the pry bar. Make sure the springs have found the right orientation with respect to the rubber pads and the metal spring perch underneath.

With the rubber pads in place, you can insert the rear spring most of the way by hand.

Use the lever again and open the space to fit the spring in. This is easier with performance springs because they are shorter when fully extended.

Install the small loop at the bottom over its guide; that's why you need the lever. Make sure the spring is well-seated in its guides before you button up.

5 Now it's time to replace the shocks. The H&R Touring Cup kit comes with new tops, so use those. But the kit does not come with new bump stops. If you're working with the original shocks, chances are good that the bump stops are severely decayed. If you're replacing replacement shocks, chances are equally good that the bump stops were discarded earlier.

In either case, you want a new set of OEM bump stops. These are absolutely critical for keeping the new shocks from becoming broken on big bumps, and the good news is that new BMW bump stops cost less than $20. You need a helper or some means of holding the shock bodies while you remove the top nuts because they tend to rotate as you work.

Tip: Cut a small amount off of the stock bump stop if the car is being lowered. Approximately 1 to 1.5 inches prevents premature engagement during cornering or large bumps on the road.

The H&R Touring Cup kit gives you these nice new shock tops to install. Bolts must be threaded through the mounting holes.

Here's the new bump stop. These cost just a few dollars, but they don't come with the kit. Buy new ones every time you change the suspension and never choose to go without them; they prevent the shock from over-compressing.

The H&R shock tops offer a much firmer bushing than stock. This is going to do a lot to tighten the rear end.

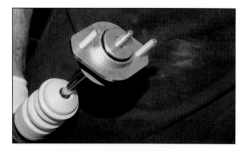

With the bolts installed, this rear shock is ready to install.

6 To install the new shocks, put the new tops on the shock bodies with the rubber bushings provided and tighten the central nut. Then insert the new shock into the tower and tighten the mounting nuts on either side. A helper is required for this job, too. Then, jack up the rear suspension to meet the bottom of the shock and attach the body to the bottom of the hub carrier. Do this on both sides and you're done.

Remember, do not use air tools to tighten the top nut.

With the new suspension and brake in place, this rear wheel well is looking very racy and works much better than the old stock units.

7 Remount the wheels. A rear wheel alignment is necessary.

Sway Bars

Sway bars dramatically affect the handling characteristics and prowess of your E36. Sway bars are designed to reduce body roll during cornering, but that's not all they do. For high-performance street cars, sway bars tuned to the application and driving style deliver substantial performance improvement.

Recall the earlier discussion about roll centers; sway bars limit the total amount of body roll, and that limits the lateral movement of the roll center. But you can't cheat physics, and the weight transfer that happens due to centrifugal force has to go somewhere, so the tradeoff is that as you increase the overall sway control evenly, you also increase lateral load transfer to the outside wheels in a corner.

You can make some decisions about sway control that will have a big effect on handling by changing the car's sway control unevenly. Depending on the relative size and setup of the two sway bars, you can adjust the car's tendency to oversteer or understeer.

Simply put, to increase understeer, stiffen the front bar or soften the rear bar. To increase oversteer,

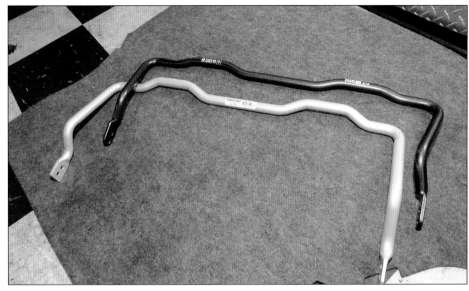

Both Whiteline and H&R make a good oversize rear sway bar. Both offer two end link installation points for some adjustment.

stiffen the rear bar and soften the front bar. In extreme cases such as rain, drivers may disconnect the rear sway bar entirely. Just remember that oversteer and understeer tendencies are affected by many factors in addition to the sway bar choice, including tire choice, alignment, roll center, and tire pressure.

You can stiffen and soften sway bars in two ways. The first and most obvious method is to use a larger, stiffer bar. The second is to change the point at which you connect the ends of the bar to the drop links.

Most sway bars are fundamentally U-shaped. The longer you make the ends of the U, the softer the bar because you have more leverage on it and more metal to flex.

Tip: A good feature in an aftermarket sway bar is a series of mounting holes for the drop link. You can stiffen the bar by moving the links away from the ends of the bar, and soften the bar by moving the

That's the stock rear sway bar on the left, and then the H&R and Whiteline aftermarket options. Obviously, this project car is going to corner a lot flatter with the H&R part installed.

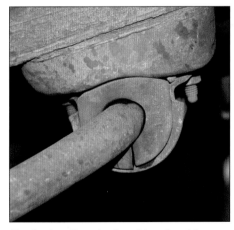

Replacing the stock rubber bushings on the sway bars is just as important as any other set of bushings in the suspension, and the same suggestions apply: anti-seize and poly bushings.

links back outward. You can switch between street and track setup just by moving the end links!

One thing to consider as you shop for sway bars is whether a given bar is hollow or solid. Hollow bars are lighter than solid bars of the same diameter, obviously. Pay attention to this: a hollow bar is not as stiff as a solid bar of the same *diameter*, but a hollow bar is stiffer than a solid bar of the same *weight* because of increased cross-section. So when making your evaluation, ask manufacturers for the percentage increase in stiffness you can expect from their bars, rather than relying on size.

The best setup for your E36 depends on your driving style and performance applications. Typically, autocrossers value a lot of oversteer when competing, and should always use an adjustable rear bar. Street-only drivers may find that the stock bars are sufficient to achieve neutral handling with a bushing upgrade. Track drivers may prefer to upgrade both bars to adjustable models and then test different settings to achieve neutral to slight oversteer. In all cases, drivers benefit from using adjustable end links on both bars.

Project: Installing an H&R Rear Sway Bar

H&R Springs makes this bar with two end-link mounting holes for easy adjustment, and includes poly bushings for rigidity. This project was performed on the project 1996 328i, but it is applicable to any E36.

Follow These Steps

1 Raise the car to a comfortable working height on the lift (or on a set of sturdy jack stands) and remove the rear wheels.

2 Remove the stock drop links at the rear control arms and at the sway bar ends. These are held on with 13-mm nuts, but they are located down in a little pocket (see photos) and you need a socket on an exten-

sion to access them. Most of this is obvious if you look at the pictures.

This is the stock drop link for the rear sway bar. With the H&R kit, you don't re-use any of this, but you might with other kits.

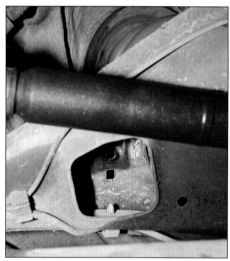

This is where the rear drop link attaches to the upper control arm.

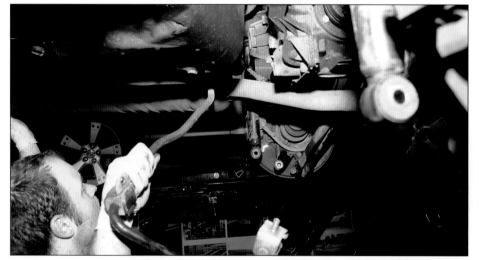

You may have to wiggle the rear sway bar a bit to remove it from the car, but it comes out easily enough. Installation is the same way. Work it into place and then it bolts right up.

You may need air tools to loosen the drop link from its attachment point on the sway bar. Lots of dirt and grime accumulate on these bolts.

3 Remove the sway bar clamps that hold the bar to the chassis. Use a socket and ratchet or wrenches to remove the clamps. You can now carefully work the sway bar out around the other components at the rear of the car.

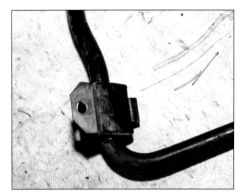

You can see that there's only one bolt that holds the clamp in place. The other side is a tab-and-slot arrangement. The new poly bushings fit in the same clamp.

4 Apply some anti-seize compound to the inside of the new poly bushings and place the bushings on the new bar. You may find it convenient to install the replacement drop link on one end of the bar at this time. Plan to route the other end through the car. Work the new bar into position carefully and reinstall the existing clamps.

The new H&R drop links are easy to install and have their own mounting ends.

5 Install the second drop link and reattach the drop links to the rear control arms using a ratchet and socket.

Tip: When you attach the stock end links or new adjustable end links to the new sway bar, use the attachment hole at the end of the

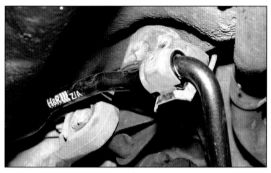

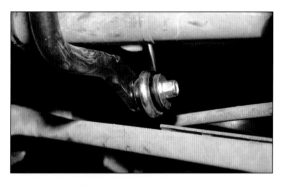

bar first. That's the softest setting. You need to get used to that before you start playing around with the stiffer setting. Upgrading the rear bar increases oversteer, and you don't want to find yourself going backward around a curve the next time it rains.

Here's the H&R rear sway bar installed with new bushings and the stock clamps. Note the anti-seize on the bushing and bar.

The H&R drop links use their own poly bushings and good strong steel for the link itself.

With the tab inserted, this sway bar clamp mount just needs its bolt threaded in to be complete.

These dual holes in the end of the sway bar allow you to change the bar's stiffness by 5 percent or so. The hole closest to the end offers the softer setting because of the greater leverage on the bar. Start with the softest setting before you move up.

Project: Installing an H&R Front Sway Bar

H&R Springs also makes this upgrade front bar with two end-link mounting holes for easy adjustment, and includes poly bushings for rigidity. This project was performed on the project 1996 328i, but it is applicable to any E36.

Follow These Steps

1 Raise the car to a comfortable working height on the lift (or on a set of sturdy jack stands) and remove the rear wheels.

2 Remove the stock drop links at the front control arms and at the sway bar ends.

This is the stock front drop link in place on the lower front control arm. You re-use the bottom mount point, but not the link itself.

Now removed, the front drop link is a simple piece. Remove the bottom mount point for re-use.

3 Remove the sway bar clamps that hold the bar to the chassis. The sway bar drops out of the car.

Unlike the rears, the front sway bar clamps use two bolts to handle the greater forces exerted by the bigger bars.

4 Apply some anti-seize compound to the inside of the new poly bushings and place the bushings on the new bar. You may find it convenient to install the drop links at this time. Move the new bar into position and reinstall the existing clamps.

A new poly sway bar bushing from H&R. Be sure to paint it with anti-seize where the bar moves.

The H&R sway bar kit comes with new drop links and poly bushings for all attachment points.

5 Reattach the drop links to the lower control arms.

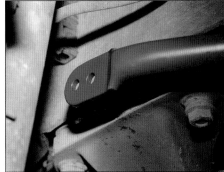

When you install the front sway bar, you may need to support the hub assembly to bring it up for easy installation.

The front sway bar is also adjustable, but this is far less important than the rear bar. In general, make the rear bar tighter and the front bar softer for increased oversteer.

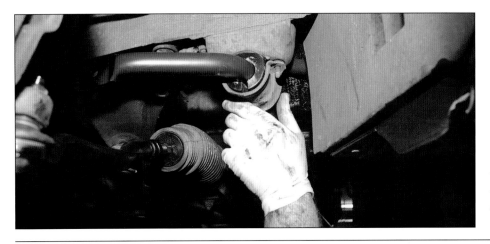

Place the front sway bar and place the bolts in the stock mounting clamps. Again, notice the use of anti-seize compound.

Adjustable Sway Bar End Links

The theory is that when a car is at rest, there is no torsion on the sway bars. This is not always true, but suppose for the moment that it is true on your car. When you climb into the driver's seat, the car is no longer standing at rest. You have compressed the left-side suspension somewhat with your weight. Now the sway bars are already pushing back on the suspension. You can relieve the preload (or set a preload of your choosing) on the sway bars if you buy adjustable drop links, which are sold by many aftermarket retailers.

Adjustable sway bar links are simple to install and use. The sway bars are wide U-shaped torsional

For the best performance of all, buy a set of adjustable drop links, and then set the sway bar preload with the car on the ground and yourself in the driver's seat.

springs. They ride above the front and rear control arms and the ends of the U are connected to the control arms with fixed-length drop links. You can remove these stock drop links easily and replace them with adjustable-length links. Then simply sit in the car and have a friend adjust them until the bar and links are about perpendicular to each other and there's no stress on the sway bars. You want the drop link to be loose, so you can turn it with two fingers. That's when there's no preload on the sway bar. Be sure to check that the sway bars and links do not bind or interfere with other components throughout the range of the suspension travel. Easy!

You can also use the adjustable links to create preload to help the car turn left or right, but improving one happens at the expense of the other, so be sure you understand the tradeoff.

Tip: If you are running coil-overs, you can't set corner weights properly unless the sway bars are disconnected.

Other Suspension Parts

Some aftermarket products offer a new fixed camber or caster setting, while others allow complete adjustability. For street use, a mild fixed adjustment is usually sufficient, while for autocross or track competition you are likely to want to be able to make your own changes. Bear in mind that if you pick a variety of products from different manufacturers, they have not been tested together and may interfere with each other.

Strut Tops and Camber Plates

The uppermost part of a strut assembly is known as the "hat" or "top mount" or simply the "strut top." This is a cap that holds the assembly together and keeps the spring compressed. One of the key functions performed by the strut top is to hold the entire strut in one position to maintain the car's stock camber setting. The strut top mounts to the car by means of three small studs that fit into holes in the car's strut tower.

BMW gave its cars comparatively soft strut top bushings to reduce NVH. The downside of this is that the strut has more play than you want in a performance setup. That's why the aftermarket has created strut tops with polyurethane or even metal bushings to reduce the play and give you more precise handling. As a bonus, you typically have a little more camber (up to -1.0 or -1.5 degrees) with aftermarket units, which helps deliver better street performance.

One popular modification is to use a device called a "camber plate" as a replacement strut top. Most coil-over kits include these as part of the kit, but replacement strut kits do not. This is simply a strut top that is adjustable, so you can set as much or as little camber as you like. Some camber plates also allow for a little bit of caster adjustment as well. This is all achieved by using slotted holes instead of a fixed bushing, so you can move the strut in relation to the strut tower.

Once you have the camber where you want it, simply tighten the adjusting bolts and the camber plates hold the strut where you want it. The tradeoff, of course, is increased NVH with any hard-mounted strut tops or camber plates.

Suspension Bushings

Most BMW buyers look for the luxury aspects of the car rather than performance, or they have quite modest performance needs. That's

As mentioned before, a fully adjustable strut top allows you to set camber and caster and hold the strut rod firmly in place.

Upgrade rear shock tops often use pillow balls like those on the top-performance front units.

This rear control arm mount bushing is made of Delrin, a nylon-like material with a great durometer hardness rating. It does not offset for camber and will likely be used with a fully adjustable strut top.

why BMW (along with every other automaker) uses soft rubber bushings throughout its cars. The downside is that these bushings don't last. They're soft to begin with, and over time they break down. So by 30,000 to 40,000 miles, the stock bushings are providing very little benefit, and allowing a lot of unwanted motion in the suspension.

You can improve the handling performance dramatically with a set of firmer aftermarket bushings, and this is usually among the first steps in suspension upgrades. There is a tradeoff, of course, and that is increased NVH with firm bushings. You may also be surprised at how responsive the steering becomes with the new bushings.

All of the control arms and sway bars on an E36 use rubber bushings to attach themselves to the chassis and hub assemblies. You want to replace these rubber bushings with a firmer material, such as polyurethane, and sometimes metal bushings can be used, even though this is generally limited to racing applications exclusively.

The technical name for these metal bushings is Heim joint, but they are also called "spherical joints," "pillow ball," or "mono-ball bushings."

These metal bushings are used in racing applications for which drivers have sacrificed all NVH concerns in favor of razor-sharp suspension responsiveness. For any other pur-

poses, these products tend to be too expensive and harsh for street use.

Heim joints incorporate pillow balls to give a more precise adjustment than is possible with stock-style ball joints or any bushing.

Project: Upgrading Rear Trailing Arm Bushings

Rear suspension performance can be improved by replacing the large rubber bushing that anchors on the forward end of the rear trailing arm pivots. The bushing itself is inset in a carrier and one large bolt holds the trailing arm in place. The forces placed on the bushing are significant, and it benefits from a snug reinforcement. An excellent time to undertake this project is when you are replacing rear springs or upgrading the bushings on the rear struts. This procedure works for all E36s.

Follow These Steps

1 Raise the car to a comfortable working height on the lift (or on a set of sturdy jack stands) and remove the rear wheels.

2 You can see where the trailing arm goes forward into the body of the car. Remove some of the plug-clips that hold the plastic trim in place and move the trim aside. You

can see the bushing carrier bolted to the underside of the body in a little pocket. Undo the three bolts that

hold the bushing carrier in place on the chassis and drop the front end of the trailing arm out of the chassis.

The rear trailing arm bushing (RTAB) is located here on the E36.

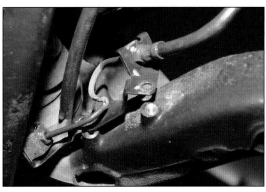

Be sure to disconnect the rear brake line holder from the trailing arm so you do not stress the brake lines during the RTAB replacement operation.

3 On the outboard side of the bushing carrier is an 18-mm bolt with a large nut. Remove that bolt; the trailing arm comes loose from the bushing carrier and you can see the bushing.

4 A special tool is required to press the bushing out of the trailing arm. The tool costs $60 to $100 to purchase, and some businesses ask more than that for rental! Ask around your community. Someone is likely to have one you can borrow.

This tool costs between $60 and $100 to purchase, and sometimes more than that to rent. See if you can borrow one through the local BMW club, because you need it to do this job.

The old and the new RTABs. You can see the difference between the old stock unit and the new poly bushings with a steel insert.

5 Be sure to put a liberal coating of anti-seize compound on the housing and on the center bore of the new bushing halves before you put the bushing in. Grease does not work because it dries out and wears away. Real anti-seize is a much better choice. The bushing must be well lubricated, otherwise it binds and causes poor ride quality and handling.

Buy a big jug of anti-seize if you're going to replace the whole suspension, and use it every time. You'll thank yourself the next time you need to work on those parts.

Just paint the anti-seize compound on any surface where parts are going to rub together. This reduces squeaking and helps prevent rust-welding of parts that are tightly held together, like ball joints.

6 Poly bushings come in two halves with a steel cylinder that fits snugly in the center. One side of the bushing can be pushed in by hand. Unlike the stock rubber bushings, the poly bushings have an outer lip. If you are considering a bushing retainer, it cannot be used with the poly bushings; the poly bushings are a better solution. For the outer half of the new poly bushing, use the bushing removal tool with a steel plate to press the bushing into place. Then insert the steel core cylinder.

You need to use the bushing puller with a metal plate to pull the new poly bushing into place.

Once the bushing is in place, put the bushing carrier back on and torque the bolt.

7 Replace the bushing carrier and the 18-mm retaining bolt. Once installed, torque the 18-mm bolt to 74 ft-lbs and then reassemble the trailing arm onto the chassis.

8 Perform the same procedure on the other side of the car. Replace the rear wheels and lower the car to the ground. Bounce the car lightly as you roll it forward and back a few feet. Replace the plastic trim and its clips.

Install the trailing arm with the new bushing. You may need to use a screwdriver to line up the holes for the bolts.

Project: Upgrading Rear Lower Camber Arms

A small amount of camber adjustment is available in the rear wheels with the stock suspension, but the lower rear control arms are very limited. It is possible to achieve additional adjustment with a set of adjustable lower rear camber arms. This procedure works for all E36s.

Follow These Steps

1 Raise the car to a comfortable working height on the lift (or on a set of sturdy jack stands) and remove the rear wheels. You can see the lower camber arms coming from the center of the car out to the bottoms of the rear hub uprights. The inboard mounting points are on the rear subframe that also houses the final drive unit.

2 A single bolt holds the inboard end of the camber control arm

Here is the Turner Motorsports control arm next to the stock unit. The Turner part looks better and offers more adjustment and easier adjustment than stock.

This eccentric bolt allows a little bit of camber adjustment on the stock lower rear control arm. I replace that with a better solution for more adjustability.

to the rear subframe. Undo that bolt. You can also undo the adjustment bolt at the outboard end. The control arm comes right out.

3 Place the stock bar on the ground and adjust the new bar to the same length, measuring center to center on the bolt holes.

The end of the Turner control arm grips the hub assembly. You can see the threaded adjustment. Simply loosen the lock nut at the top of the picture and turn the nut by the forked end to lengthen or shorten the arm.

Here's the inboard end installed in the rear subframe. No special tools or disassembly are needed.

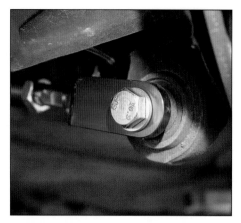

Here's the outer end installed around the hub assembly mount point. Once installed, take the car for an alignment.

4 Install the new bar and tighten it. Immediately take the car for a suspension alignment to set the rear camber.

Wheels and Tires

Everyone likes a nice set of wheels. They are among the first thing anyone notices about a car, and therefore style is important. But all wheels are not created equal. You want to select performance wheels for much more than just their looks. That begins with the overall wheel diameter, and also includes wheel width, offset, and the structure. If you plan on performance driving, you want a strong wheel that is also as lightweight as possible. Fortunately, hundreds of options bring together all those values and look great at the same time.

Start with the basics. The wheels and tires make your car's only connection with the pavement. All of your acceleration, braking, and steering go through the wheels and tires, and all the bumps and bounces come back to you through the tires and wheels. Your selection of wheels (and most important, your selection of tires) is critical to getting good performance out of everything you've done so far.

Most performance enthusiasts who compete in autocross or engage in track day activities keep at least one set of wheels and tires that are exclusively devoted to that purpose. There's no sense in taking the everyday tires off their wheels and replacing them for a track day, and you want to keep the track-day tires free

I used Falken Azenis tires on the project 328i for track and street use. This is a great performance tire with plenty of rubber for maximum grip.

BMW-Approved Wheel and Tire Sizes

Here are some of the basic considerations to evaluate when you're shopping for wheels and tires. The 1996 and later E36 models are fitted with ASC+T stability and traction controls. If you wish to use this system (and it's a good idea to use the system in any street car) you cannot use different-sized front and rear wheels and tires. The system interprets this as wheelspin and responds. Use one of the standard wheel/tire sizes in the table below to maintain normal operation of the ASC.

Wheel Size (inches)	Wheel Offset (inches)	Tire Size
15 x 6	42	185/65R15
15 x 7	47	205/60R15
15 x 7	35	225/55R15
16 x 7	45	225/50R16
16 x 8	45	225/50R16
17 x 7.5	41	215/45R17
17 x 7.5	41	225/45R17
17 x 8	47	225/45R17
17 x 8.5	41	235/40R17
18 x 8.5	35	225/40R18

A stock 15-inch 328i wheel (right) sits next to a much nicer 17-inch E46 wheel (left). Using stock BMW wheels means you can be sure that the offset is within the specified range and the wheel fits, but stock wheels tend to be heavy.

of the oil and road hazards that the street tires pick up.

Probably the most common stock wheel delivered with E36 cars is the 15-inch delivered on 325 and 328 models. The stock tire for this wheel measures 205/60-15 with a 4.8-inch sidewall and 24.7-inch diameter. This tire undergoes 817 revolutions per mile. The most common performance option would be to switch to a 17-inch wheel as used on the M3. The stock 215/45-17 tire has a 3.8-inch sidewall and 24.6-inch diameter. This tire undergoes 808 revolutions per mile. You can see that these are not very different in overall size; the increased wheel diameter is exchanged for lower sidewall height. As long as you stick with generally approved tire sizes you can keep the speedometer accurate to within 1 mph or so.

Tip: The most popular budget performance mod is to use four of the M3 rear wheels on the car. That way you have the widest wheels of the E36 line and they are still stock.

See Chapter 7 for information on modifications to your car's rear axle, but you can make minor adjustments to the car's final drive ratio by changing tire size up or down by one size. The wheel/tire combo affects acceleration because the total diameter of the tire affects the final drive ratio; a taller tire is just like a taller gear. There's a tradeoff between acceleration performance and top speed inherent in the diameter of the wheel and tire combination you choose, and the total diameter of the tires also affects the roll center a little bit.

It is not often done, but it is possible to make larger changes to the car's final drive ratio by drastically reducing tire diameter. For example,

The E36 M3 wheels I chose for the Falken Azenis performance tires. On the M3, the rear wheels are wider than the fronts.

The basic E36 wheel is a good part, but the availability of performance tires in 15-inch sizes is dwindling. Plus, a bigger wheel is just going to look better overall.

Wheel Strength

The variety of wheel styles available on the market has never been greater than today, but be aware that not all wheels are equally strong. If you plan on doing some hard cornering, know that you can put a great deal of stress on the wheels. You want the wheels to be strong enough not to flex or break under cornering, and you also want them to be light. To achieve that end, look for wheels with many spokes, preferably designed in a web pattern. These are popular with racers for their light weight and strong design.

This good strong wheel design allows plenty of air to flow through, but the many spokes keep this wheel stiff and in place.

if you could find a 205/30-15 tire, the contact patch would be about the same as stock, but the diameter would be just 19.8 inches. With that tire the speedometer would be optimistic by 19.6 percent, showing 60 mph when you were actually traveling at 48 mph. The advantage to using smaller tires to change final drive is that you can easily swap back to normal size tires for street use.

Wheel Selection

Selecting wheels should be fun because you make a personal statement about your car through the wheels you select. Most E36-specific retailers know the fitment issues on wheels that they sell. A general-purpose wheel and tire shop may not. Another good source for this information is the Internet. The

E36 forums have archived information or current experience with the fitment of a wide variety of wheels.

Keep these factors in mind when selecting wheels:

• Will the inner diameter of this wheel clear my brakes, struts,

tie rod ends, and any aftermarket parts I plan to put on in the future?
• Will the outer diameter of this wheel, plus the tire I plan to run, clear my fender wells? Even if I lower the car?
• Is the width of this wheel suitable for the tires I plan to buy?
• Is the width of this wheel suitable for my car's suspension and wheel wells?
• Does this wheel have an offset within the workable range for my car?
• Is this wheel strong enough for my purposes?

Wheel Weight

As you know, wheels are unsprung weight, and you want to keep that under control. Stock 15-inch BMW alloy wheels weigh about 16 to 20 pounds apiece. The 17-inch wheels generally weigh about 19 to 22 pounds each. Things take a big jump when you go to 18-inch and 19-inch wheels, which range from 23 to 30 pounds apiece. Remember that stock wheels are selected by the automaker, and they don't want to have to replace broken wheels under warranty. Aftermarket wheels are often lighter than the stock wheel of a

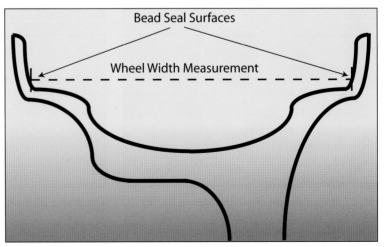

Bead Seal Surfaces
Wheel Width Measurement

This cross-section drawing shows where to measure wheel width. Go to the inside sealing surface, not the outside.

given size, but not always. It pays to ask before you buy.

Wheel Diameter

Wheel diameter is probably the first thing you need to decide. E36 models come with 15-inch through 17-inch factory options. Wheel diameter is measured as the distance across the center of the wheel from bead sealing surface to bead sealing surface, not from the edges of the rim. Measuring from the edges of the rim can add an inch or more to the measurement.

The minimum wheel size is usually dictated by the brake plans, and occasionally by the tires you want to run. Most brake kits state the minimum specs for wheel diameter, but bear in mind that this is no guarantee that a particular wheel of the specified diameter fits over a particular brake. Offset and wheel structure come into play as well. There's no test better than fitting the actual wheel/tire over the brake in the fender and checking for interference throughout the steering travel range.

Tip: Many brake kit manufacturers can provide you with something called a 1:1 caliper sweep. It is an actual-size drawing of their brake kit profile that can be printed out and test-fit against the wheel.

Wheel Width

The next factor to consider is wheel width. This is defined as the distance across the width of the wheel from bead sealing surface to bead sealing surface, again not from the edges of the rim. Measuring from the edges of the rim can add half an inch or more to this measurement.

Wheel width is a critical consideration in conjunction with the tires

The Physics of Wheels

Moment of inertia has nothing to do with the amount of time it takes you to get off the couch, but it has a lot to do with accelerating the car. Moment of inertia is a measurement of how much torque it takes to accelerate an object in angular rotation around an axis (to spin a wheel, for example).

Without breaking out the physics textbook, a small wheel takes less energy to spin up than a large wheel of the same mass because the mass is concentrated close to the axis of rotation. This is why pure racing clutches are made so small to help the engine spin up faster. It's also why 20-inch and larger wheels (rarely seen on E36s) are bad for both acceleration and braking performance. It takes more effort to get that wheel rolling, and it also takes more effort to stop it once it's going!

To use an extreme example, monster trucks need huge, torquey engines in large part to move those giant tires, but the vast majority of E36s are rolling on wheels of 17 inches or smaller. The differences in moment of inertia are tiny, between 15 and 17 inches. So don't worry about going to 17 or even 18 inches to clear the big brake kit. It's no big deal.

Next, the wheels and tires are the biggest contributors to the car's unsprung weight. Remember that unsprung weight stresses the suspension and shocks. You don't have to buy the absolute lightest wheels and tires on the market, but be aware of weight when making your selections. You'll be surprised how heavy some wheels are, especially the stock wheels.

you're selecting. A tire uses air pressure to keep its lips sealed against the wheel (called the bead seal), and if the tires are too narrow and the wheels too wide, the lips are stretched to meet the beads. This can lead to tires coming off of the bead at high speed or during cornering, which can be disastrous. Conversely, if the tires are too wide and the rims are too narrow, the tire is forced to balloon out from the rim and you have bad handling and a bad bead seal. In general, plan for the wheel width to roughly match the tread width of the tires.

The tire retailer should be able to tell you if you have a width problem. But again, the best test for wheel width it to put one on your car and move the steering and suspension through its full range of motion while checking for rubbing.

Wheel Offset

Wheel offset is the last critical dimension to look at when selecting wheels: the distance between the back of the torque circle (the surface where you bolt the wheel to the hub) and the measured center of the wheel width. A wheel with positive offset has the torque circle outboard of the centerline of the wheel width. Negative offset is where the torque circle is inboard of the centerline, and zero offset is where the torque circle is on the centerline.

Correct offset is important to ensure that the wheels clear the brakes and to avoid fender rubbing. All stock BMW wheels are designed with positive offset of +35 to +47 millimeters. That's only 12 millimeters (less than 1/2 an inch) of difference between the high and low limits. In

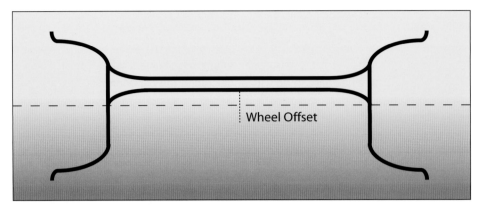

This drawing shows where to measure wheel offset. All BMW wheels fall within a narrow range of offsets.

general, wheels of greater width carry a lower positive offset.

People who change from stock wheel offset do so to accommodate wider tires. The difference in 15-inch wheels is most dramatic. If you select 205/60-15 tires, you can use a wheel with +47-mm offset, but if you choose 225/55-15, you need to pull that back to a 35-mm offset or risk tire rub on the strut body. You can either change the offset of the wheel, or if wheels are already purchased, consider a 5- or 10-mm wheel spacer.

In general, if you keep the wheel offset pretty close to stock for the diameter of wheel and the tire size you're using, you shouldn't have wheel clearance problems. If you are too far out of tolerance range, you are likely to have rubbing problems. If you are in doubt, borrow a wheel and tire of the same offset and size for a test fit on your car.

A related term you might hear is *backspacing*. Backspacing is simply the distance from the wheel's mounting face to the inboard edge of the wheel. If you select much wider wheels than stock, you need to check the backspacing in addition to the offset to make sure that the wheel won't rub on the struts or on the inner fender wells when you turn. Obviously, offset affects backspacing.

Wheel Spacers

Track is the measurement between the centerlines of the tires, or the width of your car's stance. You can add a bit of track by changing the wheel offset (see below) or by using wheel spacers. Spacers are simply big thick plates that fit between the brake rotor and the wheel.

Increasing your car's track overall helps with stability in cornering by reducing lateral load transfer. Put simply, it's easier to tip over a narrow, tall box than to tip a short, wide box. Increasing the track on either end of the car reduces that end's tendency to slide, so track is another place you can dial in oversteer or understeer.

The tradeoff with front wheel spacers is that it takes more effort to steer the car. As a result, you are increasing the length of the lever pressing on the lug bolts or studs, the wheel bearings, and the whole suspension when you're cornering. If one of the front tires is out of balance, it shakes the steering wheel more, and you increase bump steer (if you have that problem). You might also experience tire rub against the fenders in hard cornering. Also, if the wheels are offset to the outside, the effect can make the steering feel far more numb or unresponsive.

The tradeoff with spacing out the rear wheels is that you reduce over-

steer, which you've probably been trying to promote with other suspension changes. Overall, you feel bumps more acutely because you've increased the leverage working on the suspension.

As a rule, you're pretty safe with the 5-mm spacers. The 12-mm spacers are the thinnest spacers that include hub-centric rings. Avoid the 7.5- and 10-mm spacers; they do not center on the hubs.

Warning: Wheel spacers are usually used in concert with wheel stud kits, but some kits come with extra-long lug bolts instead. Whatever you choose, you must use a longer bolt or stud than the stock E36 part to replace the threaded length lost to the spacer. If you don't lengthen the lug bolts, you do not get full insertion into the hub and, sooner or later, the wheel breaks off in a corner. Probably sooner.

You should choose wheel spacers under four conditions:

- If you have installed brakes that interfere with the wheel spokes
- If you have changed the wheel back spacing and you need to move the wheels outward
- If you're autocrossing and need the stability for cornering
- If you just want a wide and pugnacious stance for aesthetic reasons on a car that is not driven often

Tip: Always use hub-centric spacers with your E36. These spacers have a raised boss similar to the boss on the stock hub, which centers the wheels around the axis of rotation. Spacers greater than 12-mm always

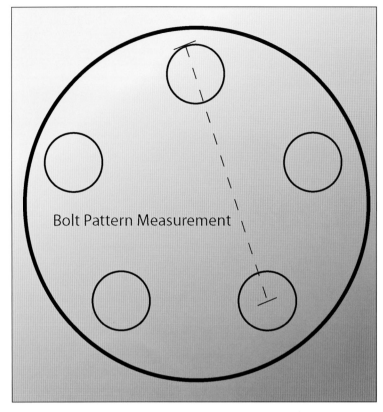

Bolt Pattern Measurement

Here's how to measure the pitch circle or bolt pattern diameter, in case you're looking at wheels and don't know if they fit or not.

German cars use lug bolts, making tire changes more annoying than they need to be. You can replace the bolts with studs for an easier installation and a truly sporty look.

come with hub bore extenders to properly center the wheels.

Bolt Pattern

BMW bolt patterns are easy to understand. All E36 models use a 5-on-120-mm bolt pattern. This means that the diameter of the bolt circle is 120 mm. This is a common bolt pattern, which means that a great variety of wheels are likely to fit your car. This measurement is also known as the pitch circle diameter (PCD).

One thing to note about BMW wheels is that the wheels are centered on the hub by a raised boss on the hub that fits into the center hole on the wheels. Some aftermarket wheels may not use the same size hub boss for location. If the hub boss does not fit the wheels, you have to rely on the lug bolts to locate the wheels, and that may not work. Hub-centric rings are frequently available for most aftermarket wheels.

Lug Bolts versus Nuts and Studs

If you are planning for serious driving, you may also want to upgrade to wheel lug studs. The lug bolts used by the factory make changing a wheel and tire more of a pain than it needs to be, and studs are an easy installation. Of course, you may not like the look of bare studs sticking out, but you can also purchase capped lug nuts. Just make sure the studs are not too long!

Studs are also useful if you decide to use wheel spacers to give yourself a little wider track. If possible, pick studs with a reinforced lower shoulder of the same depth as the wheel spacers. This helps guard against breaking a stud over time.

Tire Selection

Selecting a brand and a particular model of tire is almost a religious question. Each brand has its following, and people swear by

their favorite tires as the best. In truth, any high-quality well-known name-brand tire rated for the kind of driving you're planning to do is likely to be a good choice. Street tires today have tremendous grip, and most perform well in both wet and dry environments.

Selecting a replacement tire requires some tradeoffs. The best dry traction tires deliver greatly reduced traction on wet pavement and tend to be scary. These tires are also completely useless on gravel, snow, or ice. For most street cars, you want good all-around high-performance all-season tires because you don't want choose between swapping the wheels or going surfing every time it rains.

IMPROVING BRAKING

Most of the time, high-performance car owners focus on how to make their cars go faster; they look for torque, acceleration, top speed, and grip. But it's just as important that your E36 be able to stop as well as it goes; maybe more important. Beyond the considerations for safety, your car is more fun to drive with a really good brake system. Brakes don't cost much more than any other high-performance system on your car, and you really notice the results.

But before you dive into the brakes, remember that the stock brakes on an E36 are very good for most purposes and you can upgrade them when you need to. Generally speaking, most drivers decide to replace the brakes during their first session at a track day, because brakes that have always been more than adequate on the street will fade quickly on a racetrack.

Tip: If you are not confident of your ability to work on your own brakes, then take your car to a professional. This is one area where a screw-up can endanger others as well as yourself and your car.

Stock E36 Brake System

The E36 uses a 4-wheel disc brake system with an antilock braking system (ABS) and optionally an ASC+T stability and traction control system. The ABS relies on wheel speed sensors and includes a central pressure

Here's what it's all about. The project 328i with the Wilwood big brake kit looks great with the 17-inch wheels from the E46. I also have a set of M3 wheels for the track rubber, but they need spacers.

Here's the stock E36 328i front brake disc. It's adequate for street use when new, but this one is worn out from 112,000 miles of road driving. I'll replace it with a significant upgrade.

regulator mounted in the engine bay. This regulator can reduce brake pressure as needed to avoid brake lockup. You can still use aftermarket brake kits, but run some tests in a safe place to get used to the ABS operation with the new brakes.

The 1996 and later models may include ASC+T traction and stability control, which also makes use of wheel speed sensors and the ABS system, but this system may use the pressure regulator to actuate any brake individually, so the braking system becomes that much more complex. The 1996 and later cars also went from 3-channel ABS to 4-channel ABS. People looking for track/race use should choose the later model 4-channel ABS equipped cars because that system is far superior to the 3-channel unit.

If your car has ASC+T, the main thing that changes is that special BMW tools are required to completely bleed the brakes if the system has been evacuated of fluid, so it becomes a job for professionals. If you take care to keep fluid in the system, standard bleed procedures are adequate. You can still run aftermarket brakes, but again, you should find a skidpad and experience the ASC+T system in a safe place before you experience it on the road.

Brake Calipers

All stock E36 brakes use single-piston (also known as "single-pot") floating calipers on all four wheels. This is an important part with a distinction to make when comparing them with aftermarket systems. In a floating design, a single brake piston presses the inboard pad against the brake disc. The caliper frame is mounted on sliders, however, and the pressing action of the piston

The stock caliper is a single-piston floating design, which works well on the street and is cheap to produce. I will replace it with a fixed caliper with more swept area.

pulls the frame inward and pulls the outboard pad against the brake disc.

Most aftermarket brake systems have two, four, or six pistons, equally distributed on both sides of the caliper, and the caliper body itself stays firmly bolted in place. Stepping on the brake pedal moves all of the pistons and presses both pads against the brake disc.

Both systems deliver good braking performance, but automakers choose floating calipers because they are less expensive to manufacture. Floating calipers are also marginally easier to service.

With a fixed caliper, because the caliper body does not move and

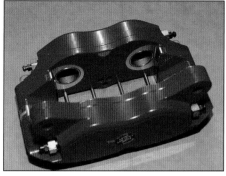

This high-performance rear caliper from Wilwood has a two-piston-per-side design that gives good clamping force on a larger pad. And because the caliper doesn't move, you have more feel through the brake pedal.

cannot flex around the slider pin, the system gives you a firmer pedal feel and better control of the rotor under braking. Virtually all aftermarket caliper upgrades are a fixed design. Most aftermarket front calipers use four pistons, with two on either side. However, the biggest and best use six pistons with three on either side. Most aftermarket rear caliper upgrades offer two or four pistons with one or two on either side of the rotor, although these are used far less often because rear brakes are simply not as important as the fronts. Rear brakes do far less of the stopping work, so the stock rear setup is often acceptable, at least

The Wilwood front caliper uses different-sized pistons with the leading end of the caliper using the smallest piston. Having a larger piston at the trailing edge helps keep the pressure equal across the whole pad face. This helps the pads wear evenly.

Here's a detailed look at a well-worn front brake disc. Even if you do a Stage 2 freshening with stock replacement rotors, this disc needs to be retired.

You can see the difference between vented and solid rotors in this side-by-side comparison. The vented rotor is on the left.

from a performance standpoint, if not a visual standpoint.

Brake Rotors

E36 disc brake rotors are made from a single piece of cast iron and machined to the specified thickness. Stock front rotors are vented, while the rears are generally solid. Exceptions exist for some years of 323i and 328i that used vented rear rotors, and of course the M3 always used vented rear brake discs.

Vented rotors are thicker and have air passages from the center of the rotor out through the perimeter of the disc. On M3 models, these air vents are curved; this makes them directional so it's very important to have the rotors on the correct side of the car. Other vented rotors use straight vents and may be used on either side of the car.

All stock E36 rotors are smooth-faced, which is to say, they are neither drilled through with holes, nor do they have grooves in the friction surface. A lot of myth goes into drilled or grooved rotors, and that myth had its basis in fact decades ago. With today's pads, however, your primary concern is that the rotor is flat,

Drilling and grooving rotors is not necessary with modern calipers and pads, but it still looks racy, so it's a popular modification.

Looking at some different vented rotors, you can see that some are substantially thicker than others, and vane designs vary widely. The rotors on the right and left have directional vanes.

Directional vanes help fling air out of the rotor, which creates a low-pressure area inside the rotor. Cool air comes in at the center near the hub and passes through the rotor before being pumped out the perimeter. More flow equals cooler brakes.

This Wilwood rear brake disc is vented and directional. The large part in the center houses the drum for the parking and emergency brake apparatus.

You can see the brake drum for the parking and emergency brake in this view of the Wilwood rear rotor. You need M3 parking brake parts to use this as designed.

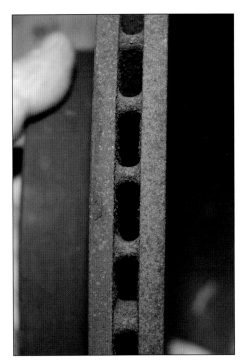

These straight vanes help push the air out a little bit, but not as much as a directionally vaned rotor does.

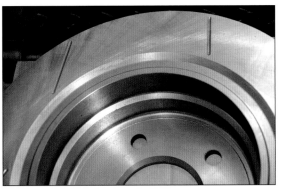

The backside of the brake rotor is machined into a crosshatch pattern that helps the brake disc engage with the pads.

Our Wilwood kit uses two-piece front rotors. The center hats are aluminum for less weight and less heat transfer.

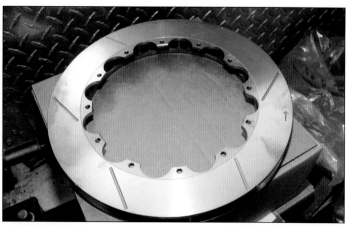

Here's the front brake rotor. It's large and well-vented, and directional. One advantage of a two-piece rotor is that this part can be replaced when worn, but you don't have to replace the center.

thick enough, and large enough to accommodate the pads. The brake rotor is a friction surface and a heat sink. Although drilling or grooving the rotor reduces unsprung weight, these modifications actually diminish the rotor's effectiveness as a heat sink.

A rotor dissipates heat in three ways. The first is radiating the heat back outward from the friction surfaces. The second is by taking the heat that's being generated on the face and moving it to the center. Cast iron has a tendency to distribute heat, so that the whole mass tends to be the same temperature. The third way is that there's a low-pressure area at the inner diameter of the rotor, and air comes in and runs through the venting vanes of the rotor. This keeps the center and the vane area of the rotor cooler than the friction surface, and the vanes expel the hot air out through the outside diameter of the rotor.

The capacity of the vanes, the surface area of the vanes, and how effectively the rotor ingests air determines how cool the center of the rotor is. By keeping the center of the rotor cooler than the friction faces, the heat is pulled away from

the friction faces. If the air going in the inner diameter of the rotor doesn't go up through the vanes and out the outer diameter, but instead seeps out through holes drilled in the face, the center will stay hotter.

The bottom line is this: Lab testing proves that cross-drilling rotors does not improve the rotor's capacity to dissipate heat. But the effect looks so sporty that most aftermarket kits not explicitly designed for racing are drilled and/or grooved. Racing rotors

tend to be smooth-faced or have only small curved slots or J-shaped indentations, which should be a clue.

Rear rotors do less work, so they are not always vented and may be used on either side of the car. In the stock E36 brake design, the rear brake discs also contain a drum brake designed to accommodate the parking brake hardware. The drum is in the center of the rear brake disc. Pulling the parking brake handle actuates a cable system that presses two

Stock Brake Rotor Sizes

This information is for all North American–market E36s.

E36 Model	Year	Front Rotor (mm)	Rear Rotor (mm)
318i	1992–1998	286, vented	280, solid
318is	1992–1997	286, vented	280, solid
323i	1998–1999	286, vented	276, vented
323is	1998–1999	286, vented	276, vented
325i	1992–1995	286, vented	280, solid
325is	1992–1995	286, vented	280, solid
328i	1996–1998	286, vented	280, solid
328i	1999	286, vented	276, vented
328is	1996–1998	286, vented	280, solid
328is	1999	286, vented	276, vented
328i Convertible	1996–1999	286, vented	276, vented
M3 (all)	1995–1999	315, vented, directional	312, vented, directional

shoes against the inside circumference of the drum, immobilizing the rear wheels. It is important to know that the parking brake assembly on M3 models is larger than for the rest of the E36 series, so if you upgrade to M3 brakes or an aftermarket kit designed for the M3, you must also upgrade to an M3 parking brake setup. You may also need to upgrade to an M3 trailing arm.

Higher-end aftermarket brake kits use rotors that are made from two pieces and dissimilar metals. The friction surface is still machined cast iron or steel, but the center "hat" portion is generally aluminum. The two halves of each rotor are bolted together. This allows you to replace the friction surface without having to replace the center. Also, cast-iron rotors expand and contract with temperature. By having a flat plate rotor mounted to an aluminum hat, you allow the rotor to expand and contract more freely, which helps keep the rotor from cracking. It's also far lighter, which reduces rotating weight.

Two-piece rotors are available in two types. One is a fixed unit (common for most kits) that is bolted together solidly and allows only marginal room for expansion. The other type is a fully floating rotor. These rotors are loose on the hub and can move in all directions. Typically, these kits are used only for race cars because they clatter while driving. Make sure to confirm that you want one kind or the other before buying the kit.

Brake Hydraulics

Every E36 uses a vacuum-assisted brake master cylinder, an antilock braking system, and hard lines throughout the chassis. The antilock system is always on; you can't turn it off, and for most purposes

you wouldn't want to. As mentioned before, your 1996 or later car may also incorporate ASC+T traction and stability control.

When you think about upgrading the brakes in your E36, realize that the master cylinder and ABS power brake system in your car have plenty of pushing power to stop the car. You don't need to upgrade these parts, and you really wouldn't want to make changes in this system for a street car. Just keep the brake master cylinder and vacuum booster in good shape and use good fresh brake fluid as recommended; they'll last for years.

Brake Bias

Auto manufacturers must find the best compromise on brake balance; one in which the brakes always work well under a variety of conditions. If you change the brakes to work at maximum efficiency under any particular scenario (including how much weight is in the car, how fast the car is traveling, the type of road surface, and how quickly do you want to stop) then you are trading off performance under other scenarios. Because you encounter so many different scenarios in real world driving, proper brake bias and design is necessarily a compromise.

Ideally, you want the braking force on the front and rear wheels to be allocated according to the weight on each pair of wheels. But, depending on how aggressively you're stopping, more weight in the car can shift forward, placing more weight on the front wheels than they have when you're accelerating. Because rear wheel lockup is especially dangerous, automakers make conservative decisions on brake bias, meaning that the stock system is usually biased to the front enough to make a full panic

stop without rear wheel lockup. Anti-lock brakes help maintain stability, but the system is still biased to put more force on the front wheels.

It is possible to have more braking efficiency under dry, smooth conditions by changing the bias. However, other variables are at work, such as the road surface and the current temperature of the brakes. So, unless you have real-time cockpit adjustable brake bias, the time and space to figure out exactly the optimum balance, and the skills to handle the results when you're wrong, you should honor the design engineers' decisions about brake bias. Furthermore, you should consider all upgrades to the brake system with an eye toward maintaining that designed-in bias.

Brake Fade

Brake fade happens when the brakes become very hot and give you less stopping power. The primary factor that contributes to brake fade is that brake pads lose their grip when they are heated past their designed range (I discuss that more later). But just as critical is the fact that the brake fluid can boil and release compressible gases when the brakes are very hot. Because the brakes depend on pressure to work, the vaporized fluid is compressed instead of the brakes squeezing the calipers. You feel this as a soft or springy brake pedal, and you don't slow down. In extreme cases, the brake pedal may go to the floor and stay there; not a good thing if you're on a racetrack headed into a corner.

It is unusual to experience brake fade when driving on public roads. BMW designed the E36 system to handle pretty much anything you can throw at it. However, if you were to ride the brakes all the way down

Stages of Brake Upgrade

Many aftermarket shops talk about brake improvements in terms of "stages." Simply put, a stage is a set of upgrades that generally go together. The higher the stage number, the greater the upgrade (and the higher the cost). You can pick the stage that works for you.

Stage 1

This is the most basic upgrade. The primary upgrade is replacing the stock brake pads with high-performance pads. Good street pads offer a little more bite and less fade when they heat up, but you can still stop on your way to work in the morning. Another good Stage 1 brake upgrade is to flush and replace the old brake fluid to fresh DOT4.

Stage 2

Includes all of the Stage 1 upgrades, plus a set of stock size replacement rotors. Common stock size replacements are made by Brembo, StopTech, and Wilwood. These are often drilled or grooved if you're looking for a racy appearance.

Stage 3

Includes all of the Stage 2 upgrades, plus a set of fixed calipers and braided stainless steel brake lines. This is really where you start to notice an improvement in braking action because the fixed calipers transmit far more feedback

This E36 M3 wheel has clearance problems with the Wilwood big brake kit. It's always better to install the brake kit before you choose the wheels.

through the pedal, allowing you to modulate the braking force more finely, keeping the brakes just on the threshold of triggering the ABS, if necessary.

Stage 4

This stage involves a full upgrade to an oversize "big brake kit" with fixed calipers. A wide variety of these kits are available, made by Wilwood, StopTech, AP Racing, Alcon, Brembo, and others. One of the considerations of these kits is that you may need to upgrade to M3 spindles and larger wheels to fit over the rotors and calipers, and you might need to change the wheel offset to fit everything under the fenders. You also need to upgrade to M3 parking brake hardware, because virtually all of these kits are designed around the M3.

Tip: It's best to buy wheels after the brake upgrades, but most people do it in the reverse order. ∎

Another look at the M3 wheels and the big brake kit. A set of 10-mm spacers will fix this, but it goes to show that you need to choose the wheels carefully.

a mountain, for example, you could induce brake fade. But if you take a car with stock brakes to a track day, you'll have brake fade within five laps, guaranteed. Racetracks really are that much harder on the equipment, even if you think you drive hard on public roads.

Brake fluid is a mixture of oils and other ingredients, designed to have a very high boiling point. Your E36 requires a Department of Transportation brake fluid standard called DOT4. Most brake fluids that you buy in auto parts stores are DOT3, so be sure to have the right fluid. Always use a fresh, sealed can of fluid when you begin. Just sitting on the shelf, an opened can of brake fluid becomes old fast, as quickly as a few hours in humid weather.

Moisture dramatically reduces the boiling point of the brake fluid. Once the brake fluid has absorbed more than 2 percent moisture content the boiling point will drop to that of water (or near it), about 212 degrees F. The term used in the industry is *hygroscopicity* to describe how likely a fluid is to absorb moisture.

Most DOT4 and DOT5.1 fluids have high hygroscopicity and need to be flushed frequently for this reason. DOT5 fluids are not nearly as hygroscopic, but are also not compatible with DOT3, DOT4, and DOT5.1 fluids. The fluid turns to gel when mixed and causes enormous damage to your car.

Hyper-exotic fluids such as Castrol SRF have very low hygroscopicity and a very high dry and wet boiling point. These give you the best of both worlds, but they also cost about $80 per liter.

When choosing brake fluid, make sure to look at the wet boiling point of the fluid to determine which one

These Hawk stock replacement pads have a slot in them to accommodate the brake pad wear sensors on the BMW.

to use; the wet boiling point is much closer to the level that the fluid will be operating at for most if its life.

When you change the brake fluid, you must be extremely careful never to let the brake fluid reservoir drain completely. This introduces bubbles into the system, and once those bubbles are in the hydraulic system, they're very difficult to remove.

For a Stage 1 brake refresh, you can use an upgraded brake fluid. Just be sure the DOT standard matches the requirements for your car.

Upgrading the Brakes

The places where you can improve your E36's braking system are at the four corners, by upgrading the flexible brake lines, calipers, pads, and rotors. As long as you stay away from the master cylinder and all the electro-hydraulic equipment, the E36 brake system is easy to work on and most people with reasonable mechanical aptitude and the right set of tools can give good results in a home garage.

A few practical factors must be considered when you think about upgrading the brakes, and those include making sure that you upgrade things in the right order and in balance, and making sure that the brakes fit under the wheels. Then you

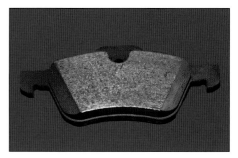

The stock rear brake pad is angled at the leading and trailing edges for smooth operation.

can move on to the fun part, thinking about braided stainless steel lines, directionally vented front rotors, then vented, slotted, or drilled rear rotors, two-, four-, or six-pot calipers, and a good pad compound.

Stage 1: Brake Pads

Upgrading stock pads to high-performance pads is the first step in achieving greater performance. The stock pads selected by any automaker are generally optimized to produce as little brake dust as possible and to last a long time while delivering braking power according to the performance level engineered for the car.

As mentioned before, when you overheat any set of brake pads past their designed range, you experience brake fade. You experience this as a mushy or springy feeling in the brake pedal, with noticeably reduced braking effect.

If you want to avoid dusting the wheels more than absolutely necessary, you need a ceramic-based pad. If you're going to take the car to a track or run autocross, you need semi-metallic. If you're going to go out and run the car longer than a 15- to 20-minute session on a racetrack, you need a full-out racing pad. You don't have a choice. There's no such thing as one pad that works well under all possible conditions.

The difference between ceramic, metallic, semi-metallic, and carbon pad compounds is mostly marketing. The material they are describing is primarily the filler material. You can have two different "ceramic" pads that provide vastly different performance because the actual friction compound mixed into the ceramic is different. No particular type of pad is superior to another, and based on the proprietary friction material they

put in, the same type of pad can yield dramatically different results. Not all ceramic pads are dust-free. The "dust-free" ceramic pads usually just have dust that is designed to be lighter in color and therefore less visible.

As a rule, any brake pad you can buy at your local auto store is a stock or OEM replacement pad. Even light sport pads are not available conventionally and must be ordered online or at a performance shop.

Tip: Most brake dust on the wheels is actually rotor material. So there's a limit to how much you can improve dusting by using different pads.

One thing to remember is that if you buy new pads, you do not want to use them on top of the friction material that has already been transferred to a used rotor. It's very important to remove that leftover material. If the rotor is in good, smooth, flat condition, taking a vibrating palm sander with 80-grit sandpaper removes the material transferred from the stock pad. If you do not remove that layer, you can significantly impair the new pad from laying down the material it wants to properly give you the performance you should have. Most people who think they have warped a rotor simply have material built up unevenly on the rotor.

Put a nice crosshatch on the rotor so that the surface is clean enough for the new pad to lay itself down. It comes off pretty readily and without much effort, just two or three minutes on each side. The most important thing is to make sure the face of the sander is flat on the rotor on both sides.

By choosing a set of high-performance brake pads, you can achieve more stopping power and more resistance to brake fade at

high temperatures. But you're usually trading off the amount and type of brake dust that is produced, and frequently, you also trade off stopping performance when the brakes are cold. Every brake pad has a heat range where it works best. High-performance brake pads are designed to work when the brakes have been heated over a few laps on a racetrack. Stock pads are designed to work through a much lower temperature range, where the discs may never become truly hot.

In common street driving, you probably won't ever reach the optimum heat range for a racing pad. This is one area where "racing parts" aren't necessarily better for your purposes. But brake pad manufacturers typically offer lines of high-performance street pads designed for your E36. If you just want more braking bite for your street car, choose a street performance pad.

To choose a particular brand of pad for your car, talk to performance experts in your area (people who drive on the same roads in the same weather in the same kind of car as you) and find out what's working for them. Be prepared to try a few different brands and find one that works well for you. In general, for street driving you want a brake pad that works well completely cold, because that's the condition for most of your street driving. You also want a low-dust pad, because you want to keep the street wheels looking good. If you plan on aggressive street driving; for example, if you drive a windy mountain road to work each day, then you should consider a pad that trades off dead cold performance for hot performance without fading. You're likely to have a little more dust with this kind of pad, but you have confident braking all the way down the hill. Just remember to take it easy until you've warmed the pads each morning!

At the racing end, you're sacrificing all other considerations for hot performance. Many people come to understand this at their first track day, when they note that their nice street pads offer no stopping power whatsoever after just two or three laps of the racetrack. That's because street pads are simply not made to slow your car from top speed several times per minute.

One thing to keep in mind is that if you go away from OEM stock pads, you are likely to lose the brake wear sensor function in your E36. There's a wire that attaches to the stock brake pads, and when they wear down, a sensor on the end of the wire triggers a light on the dashboard. You have to tie that wire and its connection fit-ting up out of the way if you change to aftermarket pads that do not support the sensor, and then monitor the brake wear personally.

Finally, whatever pad you choose for your driving habits, be sure to replace all the brake pads at the same time, to preserve the balance between the front and rear brakes. As you should expect by now, pad and rotor wear for high-performance parts is greater than for stock.

Tip: Don't make the mistake of thinking that race pads are better on the street. The fact is that racing pads must be operated at high tempera-ture to work. If you put them on a street car, they may not even stop the car when cold.

Stage 2: Rotors

Upgrading the rotors generally goes along with changing the cali-pers, and that means a full brake kit, but there are benefits to upgrading the stock rotors even if you can't afford the whole big brake kit. When it's time to freshen the brakes, you might as well spend a couple more bucks and buy a Stage 2 upgrade. You can do the job in your own garage with two people in less than an hour.

You can get more out of the brake rotors in two ways. One is to use larger rotors and the second is to use better rotors. Larger rotors have more friction surface (also known as swept area), more mass to absorb and disperse heat, and better leverage on the wheel. But a larger rotor requires an expensive aftermarket caliper and that frequently means replac-ing wheels and tires as well. So, what makes a rotor better?

You can upgrade the rotor by using a stock diameter rotor with improved venting. In all vented rotors, the air comes in through the center of the rotor and pushes out at the edge. This makes sense because you want the cool air around the bearings first, then flowing through the rotor to cool the brakes, and then leaving the area. If air flowed in from the outside perimeter, it would bring heated air to the center where it would heat the hub and ruin the bearings.

Most stock vented rotors can go on either side of the car because the vanes in between the two friction surfaces are straight and radial; they travel straight out from the center. A directional rotor has curved vanes, which act like a centrifugal pump, flinging air from the center of the rotor out through the perimeter con-tinuously as the wheel turns.

Many people install directional rotors backward, though, because they think the air flows the opposite way, scooped in from the perimeter

Reading the Numbers on Brake Pads

Every set of brake pads has a code stamped on the side of the friction pad. This is more than a part number; it tells you about the friction properties of the pad.

The tests required to assign these codes were developed by the SAE in the United States and are similar to other tests performed elsewhere around the world. The codes on foreign pads should be the same as on U.S. pads. A standard edge code begins with a three-letter brand identification code, then an alphanumeric code that references the type of friction material, two letters that specify the friction properties, and then a numeric date code that specifies when the pad material was produced.

The part of the edge code that you care about most is the friction properties code. Friction is always specified as E, F, G, or H. As you might expect, E is the lowest friction rating, while H is the highest. The first letter in the code is the pad material's cold friction rating, so that's what you have the first time you apply the brakes in the morning. The second letter is the hot friction rating, or what you have when the brakes are fully up to temperature but not overheated. Everything goes away when the pads exceed their designed heat range.

In general, high-performance pads have G or H ratings, while street pads have E or F ratings. If a set of pads does not have these ratings, you want to find out why. They may be fakes, or the manufacturer may have chosen not to partici-pate in this program.

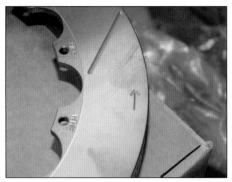

This arrow shows the forward direction of rotation for this brake disc. Always check to make sure you've installed each brake rotor on the correct side of the car.

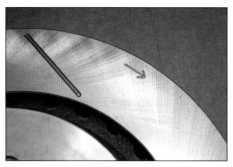

The same directional indicator on a rear brake rotor. Unless the rotor has directional vanes, you won't see these indicators. Straight vaned and solid rotors can be used on either side of the car.

and pushed toward the center. This is why curved-vane directional rotors are marked left side or right side, or they are marked with an arrow that indicates their forward rotation. It's important to install these rotors in the proper orientation so that the pumping effect works as designed. Performance Friction, Wilwood, Brembo, StopTech, and Girodisc make excellent curved-vane front rotors in solid, grooved, or drilled configuration.

Before you do anything to the brakes, buy an official factory repair manual for your specific model and year and follow all of the instructions in that manual as you work.

Stage 3: Brake Lines and Calipers

The stock flexible brake lines run from the ends of the hard lines in the wheel wells to the brake calipers. These lines need to be flexible in order to move with the wheels as you drive. The stock lines are made from a layered reinforced rubber, and they're pretty good, but they do inflate slightly when you press on the brakes. The older they are, the more they can balloon, and eventually crack. This expansion steals some

of the braking pressure and contributes to a spongy pedal feel. You can fix this with a set of braided stainless steel brake lines.

Bimmerworld and Troutman both make high-quality braided steel brake line kits for many cars, including the E36. These kits come with fresh sealing washers and any other required hardware. Goodridge also sells top-quality kits with excellent braided lines and fittings at the ends. These line sets are put together well and install as easily as OEM replacements.

Using ordinary hand tools, you can install these lines yourself in a couple of hours, and the process is included below in the big brake kit replacement procedure. You need to bleed the brakes when you're done, so be sure you have a friend to help, some fluid, wrenches that fit the bleed nipples, as well as a length of rubber hose and a receptacle for used fluid.

Tip: While you have the system open, install speed bleeders. Speed bleeders are standard metric bleed nipples with a one-way valve built in. They prevent the system from sucking air back in during the bleed

process. No special work is required; just take out the old bleed nipples and screw in the speed bleeders the next time you bleed the brakes. You can purchase speed bleeder nipples at any good automotive supply shop for about $15 per pair. These are the only things I've found in more than 25 years that really work to improve the bleeding process.

If you upgrade the calipers, be aware that you will likely have to change the brake pad format (shape and size) as well. Most aftermarket calipers use standard pad formats that are manufactured by many pad makers, but these are not necessarily compatible with the stock format.

More pistons and larger pads, improve braking efficiency by increasing your ability to squeeze the rotor, and you are also likely increasing the area of the rotor that is squeezed at any given time. Increasing the friction area gives you more stopping power.

A set of braided steel brake lines is a great investment. Rubber-based lines tend to blow up like balloons with repeated applications of brake pressure. These lines give a better brake feel.

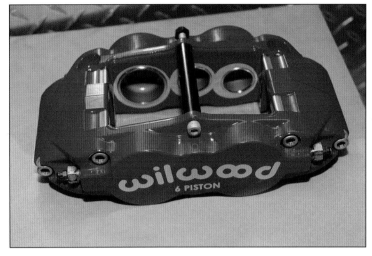

I am installing this six-piston Wilwood brake caliper for the big brake upgrade on the project 328i. It has a much larger swept area and more potential clamping force than the stock caliper.

If you are buying calipers, be sure you have both a left- and a right-side unit. Most calipers are directional because they mount in the same position, but in an opposite orientation on the left and right wheels. In all cases, the bleed nipple must be on top of the caliper for it to work. If you mount a left-side caliper on the right, it is upside-down and the bleed nipple is on the bottom! Because bubbles rise to the top, you will never be able to bleed the air out of that caliper in that position.

Project: Installing a Rear Brake Kit with Upgraded Calipers

The rear brake upgrade process can be accomplished in your garage with a few guidelines.:

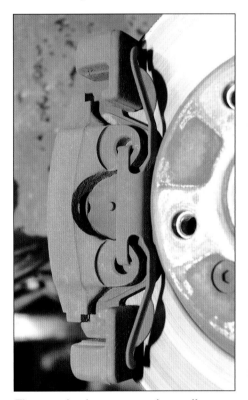

The rear brakes are much smaller than the fronts but are fundamentally the same design. You could do a Stage 1 or Stage 2 rear brake upgrade and a big brake kit on the front and the car would be okay.

Follow These Steps

1 Jack the car up and put a set of good jack stands underneath it, then remove the rear wheels. Lay out all the parts and tools you will use. Make sure you have all the tools and parts you need to complete the job, including a supply of fresh brake fluid.

2 Undo the retaining bolt that holds the stock brake rotor to the hub. This bolt uses a 6-mm hex head fitting. If the bolt is stuck, engage the parking brake for a little more leverage. It may require some effort, heat, and penetrating oil to loosen the bolt.

3 There is a spring clip that holds the pads in place within each caliper. Pry the spring clip off of the caliper to allow the pads to move.

4 Release the parking brake if it is set.

5 Use a 7-mm hex wrench to loosen and remove the main part of the caliper from the caliper frame. Then remove the two 16-mm bolts that hold the caliper frame to the hub. The bolts are located out of sight behind the caliper. Remove the caliper from the rotor. If the rotor has significant wear, you may need to twist the caliper slightly to re-compress the hydraulic piston to clear the lip on the perimeter of the rotor.

6 Remove the brake pad wear sensor wire carefully. Do not ever cut the wire or pull the sensor from the stock pads roughly. If the sensor is damaged, the brake wear sensor light on the dashboard illuminates until you spend money to replace that sensor. The sensor unplugs from the brake pad. You may need to use a screwdriver or pliers to gently pop it free. Aftermarket brake kits do not support the use of the wear sensor, so use zip-ties to secure the sensor and its wire out of the way.

Here's a BMW brake pad wear sensor. These must be in good condition and present or you see a brake warning light on the dashboard.

7 Remove the flexible brake line from its fixed mount point in the wheel well. There is usually a spring clip that helps hold this assembly in place. You can remove the spring clip with needle-nose pliers. Then, spray the connection with penetrating oil to help loosen the threads. It is critical that you do not damage the connection or twist or crimp the hard line in any way. This area may require some cleaning, as dirt and road debris tends to collect at this fitting.

Tip: It is highly recommended that you remove and install all hydraulic lines with line wrenches. A line wrench is a five-sided wrench designed specifically for this job. Standard two-sided box end wrenches may strip the fitting, causing you some serious grief.

Tip: When you remove the flexible line, some brake fluid runs out of the open end of the hard line. Have rags or a receptacle ready to catch that fluid so it doesn't end up on the suspension and brake components. Remember that brake fluid is highly corrosive to painted surfaces! Be certain not to get it on the paint, or on your hand, which you then could put on the painted body panel to support yourself.

8 Remove the stock rotor from the hub. You may need to gently tap the rotor loose with a soft-faced mallet. It fits tightly on the hub and some rust and dust may be holding it in place. If you don't have a soft-faced mallet, use a rag over the rotor when you tap it loose.

9 You are now looking at the bare hub, and you can see the dust shield. The dust shield does not fit an aftermarket big brake kit, but it is difficult to remove without disassembling the entire rear suspension. Trim the lip off the shield with tin snips or similar tool.

The stock rear brake setup has a lip around the rear brake rotor. The oversize Wilwood rear brake rotors do not clear this lip, so you have to trim it away.

With the lip cut off, the rear hub is ready for the Wilwood big brake kit to be installed.

10 Now you can begin installing the replacement kit. Before you begin, take a moment to scuff the friction faces of the rotors with 80-grit sandpaper. Use a vibrating palm sander if you have one. Get a good crosshatch pattern into the friction surfaces. This helps them bite and wear in correctly.

11 Begin reassembly by installing the rotor. Rear rotors are not generally directional, but check to be sure. Use the same hex bolt and at least two lug bolts to affix the new rotor and center it on the hub. Pay special attention and make sure that the rotor assembly is seated properly around the central hub boss and the parking brake hardware. If you need to adjust the parking brake shoes, orient the rotor so that one lug bolt hole is at the top of the rotation (12 o'clock) and then you should be able to access the star adjuster wheel using the hole at about 2 o'clock.

Wilwood uses these custom caliper brackets to set the caliper at the correct distance from the hub so the caliper rides in just the right place.

12 One of the main reasons to choose an aftermarket brake kit is to obtain a fixed caliper, but with a fixed caliper you must set the spacing to make sure the caliper fits evenly around the rotor. Wide manufacturing tolerances affect the precise placement of the caliper mounting flange relative to the rotor face. A sliding caliper can accommodate those tolerances because it self-centers on the rotor. However, a fixed caliper has to be centered with shims. The brake kit should come with a set of bolts, spacer shims, sleeves, and washers to position the caliper relative to the mounting bracket.

Use the stock 16-mm bolts to fasten the caliper mounting bracket to the hub flange. Then snugly mount the caliper on the bracket with no shims. Insert the brake pads and rotate the rotor. You might be able to feel one pad or the other touching the rotor, but the pads should not drag. If one pad is significantly tighter than the other, it is usually the outer pad. You can insert shims between the caliper and the bracket to move the caliper outward until the pads are evenly loose around the rotor. In the event that the inner pad is too tight, you might be able to reverse the bracket on the flange to change the spacing, or you might need to machine a little material off the flange to center it.

Tip: Do not assume that the two sides of your car require the same thickness in shims. Each side must be measured and shimmed separately.

13 The caliper should also be adjusted so that the brake pad friction material comes almost to the perimeter of the rotor. Do not finalize the setup until the rotor perimeter is set correctly and you have the correct number of shims in place.

Finally, before you torque the caliper on the bracket, make sure the caliper is oriented correctly. Some aftermarket calipers have bleed valves at both the top and bottom of the caliper body so that they can be used on either side of the car, while others have one or two bleed valves that must be positioned at the upper end. If you install the caliper with the bleed valve pointing down, you can never remove the air out of the caliper. Examine the calipers carefully and understand their proper orientation before you install.

The Wilwood rear caliper has a bleed valve on each end so that you can install it in any orientation and still bleed the brakes successfully.

Here's the Wilwood rear brake installed and ready to go. It looks great and works great. You need to upgrade to M3 parking brake hardware if you install this kit on a 325, 328, or 323.

14 The brake fluid inlet hole on each caliper is usually covered with a removable cap. Remove the cap and install the flex line. Install the flex line fitting so that the line leaves the caliper pointing out and up when the caliper is in its installed position. Always use the new sealing hardware that comes with the flex line kit. The banjo bolt crush washers are one-time use only. If you have to remove the bolt you need to source new ones! The brake system operates at upwards of 1,200 psi. You do not want a leak in this location!

15 When you have the shims set up correctly, torque the caliper to the mounting bracket according to the manufacturer's torque spec. Use a good torque wrench and some Loctite or other thread sealant.

16 Now, connect the flex line to the hard line. Use zip-ties if necessary to secure the line to the stock installation locations. Feed the flex line up to the hard line and, once again, use the line wrench to snug the hard line connection to the flex line. Use the stock spring clip to secure the connection.

17 Perform the same steps on the opposite side of the car. Then, when all of the new components are installed, refill the fluid reservoir and bleed all four brakes until no air bubbles are in the system.

18 Put the wheels back on your car and carefully check for clearance. This is not generally a problem with rear brakes, but it is often an issue with front brakes.

When you're all done, take it easy on the new brakes for a while. Even the best brakes need a couple hundred miles to really bed-in and work their best.

The E36 M3 wheels offer plenty of clearance in the rear. No spacers are needed back here.

Stage 4: Big Brake Kits

When you're ready to go all the way, it's time for a big brake kit on your E36. Depending on the kit you choose and the current wheel size, you might even need to buy new wheels and tires at the same time to clear the new binders.

Many kits with rotors and calipers of different sizes and configurations have been adapted to the E36. The advantages of a big brake kit are numerous; you have better leverage, more pressure on the pads, bigger pads, more swept area, directionally vented rotors, and your choice of high-performance pad compounds. Plus, they look great, especially if you have some nice open wheels to show off the kit. There aren't too many downsides to a big brake kit, but depending on the kit, you might sacrifice a little extra unsprung weight. And, of course, there's the expense. A big brake kit just for the front wheels can cost up to $3,000, plus installation.

One good option is to upgrade to M3 specifications, and kits cost about $2,000 for this upgrade, including all required parts. If you buy an aftermarket kit, you need to source M3 spindles (also known as king pins) separately to make the kit fit the basic E36. The offset for the caliper mounting flange is different on the M spindle, and the calipers do not line up correctly without these parts. The BMW part numbers you're looking for are 34 11 2 227 907 for the left side spindle, and 34 11 2 227 908 for the right side spindle. These may be sourced from junkyards, eBay, or from performance suppliers.

The main consideration when you're thinking about a brake kit is much the same as for all the individual components: Will this kit work with the kind of driving you're going to do? Even if you plan on street driving only, chances are you'll love a big brake kit, provided you choose a good street pad and not a racing pad.

A high-quality big brake kit is not hard to find. If you're working on any E36, except for an M3, be aware that you will likely have to source M3 spindles and hubs. The spindles on the M3 have a greater offset for the caliper mount and the aftermarket manufacturers designed for that spindle only.

I installed this massive Wilwood big brake kit on the project 328i. With this much brake, I never worry about brake fade on the track.

It's generally best to buy a kit when upgrading to big brakes because the hard work of building everything to line up correctly has already been done for you. You can purchase front, rear, or all-around big brake kits from Wilwood, StopTech, AP Racing, and Brembo. All of these are good choices and feature high-quality components. Your decision factors are size, price, and capability.

Choosing the size of the brake kit affects your ability to use various wheels. Generally speaking, any big brake kit requires at least 17-inch wheels. But not all 17-inch wheels are the same, and yours may also require spacers or they may not fit at all. It's best to choose brakes before choosing wheels, for that reason, and test fit any wheels before you buy.

Pricing is an obvious concern, and goes hand in hand with capability. Generally speaking, the more expensive the kit, the better the

stopping power (and the less fade in track use). Kits that use larger rotors and calipers continue to stop your car long after the stock system or smaller kits have faded. But this is a consideration only for track use, or if you have a habit of descending very long, steep hills with slow corners. As a general rule, you don't need the biggest brake kits for street use; any kit with fixed calipers offers as much braking as you will ever need on the street, provided you choose a good street brake pad.

Top kits, such as the Wilwood setup that I chose for this project car, use two-piece rotors and extra large six-piston front calipers, and upgraded single-piece rotors in the rear to preserve the parking brake function. You also have to source M3 parking brake components if you're upgrading a 325 or 328.

As with any mature aftermarket, all of the major respected brands

produce a good product. StopTech offers kits with two-piece front rotors up to 355-mm diameter by 32-mm thick, and 332-mm by 32-mm in the rear. That full four-wheel kit costs more than $5,000, and does not offer parking brake functionality, but it is an excellent track or racing setup. Brembo offers a 355-mm and 332-mm kit, or a slightly smaller 320- by 28-mm two-piece front rotor kit, with its excellent Brembo Monobloc calipers. Brembo rear brake kits are 328-mm with two-piece rotors.

AP Racing offers a 325- by 32-mm or 330- by 28-mm front disc brake kit, with its racing four-piston calipers, for about $2,600. One advantage to AP Racing kits is that the calipers are not painted or powder coated. They are anodized with a nice gray finish that is tougher than paint or powder, so it looks better even after a long period of hard use.

Project: Installing a Wilwood Big Brake Kit

You can do this job in your own garage. This project installed a set of Wilwood rotors, four-piston front calipers, a set of braided stainless brake lines, and a set of Wilwood rear brakes. I chose Wilwood for the company's excellent reputation and ready parts availability. The mechanical procedure is substantially the same for any aftermarket brake kit.

With any brake kit of this size, you need to think ahead for wheel fitment issues. The stock 15-inch E36 wheels no longer fit after you install these brakes. You also need a supply of safety wire and safety wire pliers to do this job correctly.

With any aftermarket big brake kit, you lose the functionality of the stock brake pad wear sensor. If you

install aftermarket brakes, you must take responsibility for monitoring your own pad and rotor wear.

Tip: Before you do anything to the brakes, buy an official factory repair manual for your specific model and year and follow all the detailed instructions in that manual. Furthermore, always follow the printed instructions that come with the brake kit.

Follow These Steps

1 Aftermarket two-piece rotors are not generally assembled for you, and the bolts must be safety-wired. Some manufacturers offer an option to have the rotors pre-assembled. But if yours require assembly, begin by putting the brake

rotors and "hats" together according to the manufacturer's torque specifications. The torque value to affix the rotor to the hat is measured in inch-pounds rather than foot-pounds. This is a critical distinction. Do not over torque these parts. As a rule, the fasteners are one-time-use parts.

These small Torx bolts hold the two-piece front rotors together.

When assembling the two-piece rotors, remember that the center hats are aluminum. The bolts are tightened in inch-pounds; be careful with the torque wrench.

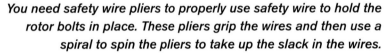

You need safety wire pliers to properly use safety wire to hold the rotor bolts in place. These pliers grip the wires and then use a spiral to spin the pliers to take up the slack in the wires.

It takes some practice to be proficient with safety wire pliers, but follow the directions in the Wilwood kit and give yourself some time. You'll get the hang of it.

Safety wiring looks professional and really helps keep the rotor bolts in place. Just clip the wires if you ever need to replace the friction surface of the rotor.

2 Jack the car up, put a set of good jack stands underneath it, and then remove the front wheels. You can see the entire stock brake system clearly. Note the caliper and pads, rotor, flexible brake line, and the brake wear sensor wire that is attached to one of the inboard brake pads. Lay out all the parts and tools you will use and make sure you have all the tools and parts you need to complete the job, including a supply of fresh brake fluid.

3 Take a moment now to undo the retaining bolt that holds the stock brake rotor to the hub. This screw uses a 6-mm hex head fitting. Use a socket and ratchet to remove it because this gives you much greater leverage. Because of the dust and heat cycling, these bolts are often hard to loosen. If the bolt is stuck, apply heat and penetrating oil. Then place a screwdriver into the vanes around the perimeter of the rotor to hold it tightly. It may require some effort to loosen the retaining bolt.

To begin the project, I removed the wheel and exposed the stock front brake. You remove the caliper first, but you could just remove the whole assembly if you are going to upgrade to M3 spindles.

4 A spring clip holds the pads in place within each caliper. Pry the spring clip off the caliper to allow the pads to move.

To remove the front brake for a Stage 1 to Stage 3 upgrade, first remove the spring clip that holds the outer pad in place.

5 Use a 7-mm hex wrench to remove the two bolts that hold the main part of the caliper to the caliper frame. Then use a 16-mm wrench to remove the caliper frame from the spindle flange. The bolts are located out of sight behind the caliper. Remove the caliper assembly from the rotor. If the rotor has significant wear, you may need to twist the caliper slightly to re-compress the hydraulic piston to clear the lip on the perimeter of the rotor.

6 Remove the brake pad wear sensor wire carefully. Do not ever cut the wire or pull the sensor from the stock pads roughly. If the sensor is damaged, the brake wear sensor light on the dashboard illuminates until you spend money to replace that sensor. The sensor unplugs from the brake pad. You may need to use a screwdriver or pliers to gently pop it free.

Aftermarket brake kits do not support the use of the wear sensor, so use zip-ties to secure the sensor and its wire out of the way. If you leave the sensor attached but zip-tied out of the way the light does not trigger. If you unplug the sensor it triggers the light.

7 Remove the flexible brake fluid line from its fixed mount point in the wheel well. A spring clip usually helps hold this assembly in place. Use needle-nose pliers to remove the spring clip. Then, spray the connection with penetrating oil to help loosen the threads. Use a 17-mm wrench on the flex line and an 11-mm line wrench to loosen the hard line connection. It is critical that you do not damage the connection or twist or crimp the hard line in any way. This area may require some cleaning, as dirt and road debris tend to collect at this fitting. If you live in an area where the roads are salted, it is possible that the fitting is rusted onto the hard line. If this is the case, and the fitting turns but also twists the hard line, stop immediately. You do *not* want to twist the fitting off of the hard line because it requires some very expensive repairs. Go see your local professional. The main thing is to just make sure that when the fitting is turning, the hard line is not!

Tip: When you remove the flexible line, some brake fluid runs out of the open end of the hard line. Have rags or a receptacle ready to catch that fluid so it doesn't end up on the suspension and brake components.

Here is the flex line that you change as part of the brake upgrade. A set of line wrenches helps loosen this part without damaging the hard line.

8 Remove the stock rotor from the hub. You may need to gently tap the rotor loose with a soft-faced mallet, because it is a tight fit on the hub, and some rust and dust may be holding it in place. Penetrating oil at the lug bolt holes and around the hub boss may help.

9 You are now looking at the bare hub, and the dust shield. You do not need to remove the front dust shields, because they do not wrap around the edges of the stock rotors.

Here's the front hub with all the brake components removed. You can discard the brake dust shield if you like, but it's useful on a street-driven car.

10 Connect the new flex lines to the fixed mount up in the wheel well. In some cases, you must use a drill to increase the size of the hole in the fixed mount to the hydraulic hard line. Protect the hard line and fitting if you need to drill, and be careful.

11 Now you can begin installing the replacement kit. Before you start, take a moment to scuff the friction faces of the rotors with 80-grit sandpaper. Use a vibrating palm sander if you have one. Get a good crosshatch pattern into the friction surfaces. This helps them bite and wear in correctly.

If you are upgrading an M3, you can install the Wilwood kit directly onto the existing hub and spindles. If you are installing on any other E36, you need to acquire a set of M3 spindles. These spindles are identical to other E36 spindles, except that they provide more room for larger calipers and rotors.

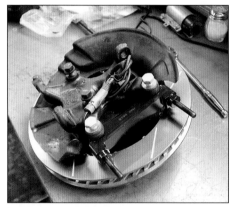

For the proper offsets for the big brake kit, I needed to buy M3 spindles. Without them, the rotors and calipers do not line up correctly.

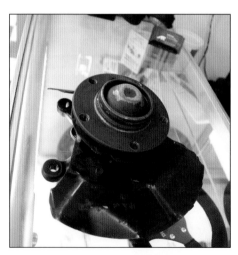

The M3 spindles were obtained from a junkyard, so they came with the hubs and everything pre-assembled. I replaced the bearings just to be on the safe side.

12 Begin reassembly by installing the rotor. If the aftermarket rotors are directional, pay attention to which side has which rotor. If you have a two-piece rotor, make sure that all of the fasteners holding the rotor to the hat are installed according to the manufacturer's directions.

Install the rotor onto the hub. Use the same hex bolt and at least two lug bolts to affix the new rotor and center it on the hub. Pay special attention and make sure that the rotor assembly is seated properly around the central hub boss.

You can see the bolt coming through the near side of the caliper. That's the caliper mounting bracket for the front rotors. You can also see the directional vanes in the rotor.

With the Wilwood rotor installed, the next step is to mount the caliper and shim it, if necessary, and then center it on the rotor.

13 One of the main reasons to choose an aftermarket brake kit is to obtain a fixed caliper. But, with a fixed caliper, you must set the spacing to make sure the caliper fits evenly around the rotor. Wide manufacturing tolerances affect the precise placement of the caliper mounting flange relative to the rotor face. A sliding caliper can accommodate those tolerances because it self-centers on the rotor. However, a fixed caliper has to be centered with shims. The brake kit should come with a set of bolts, spacer shims, sleeves, and

Test fit the caliper to make sure the rotor rides right in the middle of the space so you don't end up with a pad rubbing on the rotor surface.

washers to position the caliper relative to the mounting bracket.

Use the stock 16-mm bolts to fasten the caliper mounting bracket to the hub flange. Then mount the caliper snugly onto the bracket with no shims. Insert the brake pads and rotate the rotor. You might be able to feel one pad or the other touching the rotor but the pads should not drag. If one pad is significantly tighter than the other, it is usually the outer pad.

You can insert shims between the caliper and the bracket to move the caliper outward until the pads are evenly loose around the rotor. In the event that the inner pad is too tight, you might be able to reverse the bracket on the flange to change the spacing, or you might need to machine a little material off the flange to center it.

Tip: Do not assume that the two sides of your car require the same thickness in shims. Each side must be measured and shimmed separately.

Here's the caliper bracket for the Wilwood front brakes. The threaded holes mate to the M3 spindle, while the bolts go through the caliper body to hold it in place.

You can see how the caliper bracket mounts to the spindle and holds the caliper at a precise distance from the hub.

14 The caliper should also be adjusted so that the brake pad friction material comes almost to the perimeter of the rotor. Do not finalize the setup until the rotor perimeter is set correctly and you have the correct number of shims in place.

Finally, before you torque the caliper on the bracket, make sure the caliper is oriented correctly. Some aftermarket calipers have bleed valves at both the top and bottom of

the caliper body so that they can be used on either side of the car. Others have one or two bleed valves that must be positioned at the upper end. If you install the caliper with the bleed valve pointing down, you can never remove the air from the caliper. Examine the calipers carefully and understand their proper orientation before you install.

15 The brake fluid inlet hole on each caliper is usually covered with a removable cap. Remove the

cap and install the flex line. Always use the sealing hardware that comes with the flex line kit. Install the flex line fitting so that the line leaves the caliper pointing out and up when the caliper is in its installed position.

16 When you have the shims set up correctly, torque the caliper to the mounting bracket according to the manufacturer's torque spec. Use a good torque wrench and some Loctite or other thread sealant.

17 Perform the same steps on the opposite side of the car. Then, when all of the new components are installed, refill the fluid reservoir and bleed the front brakes until no air bubbles are in the system.

I use Wilwood fluid with the Wilwood brake kit. It's the right stuff, rated for racing, and I know it does not damage the calipers.

The Wilwood kit comes with several bottles of brake fluid. Don't open more than you need for installing the kit and filling and bleeding the system. You can use the rest later.

18 Put the wheels back on the car and carefully check for clearance. You may find that stick-on balancing weights on the inner wheel hit the caliper. Pull them off and take the car to have the wheels bal-anced with the weights elsewhere on the wheel.

You may have to address a range of minor fitment issues with after-market products. Manufacturing tolerances frequently require some thought and adaptability to line up everything correctly. This is different from forcing a part that simply

These H&R 5-mm spacers are made for BMW cars and are a good choice. Universal spacers are never as good.

does not fit. Usually, a thin washer or a little grinding makes a part fit the car correctly.

When you're all done, take it easy on the new brakes for a while. Even the best brakes need a couple hundred miles to really bed in and work their best.

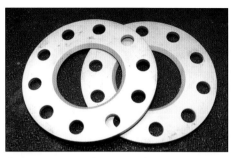

Spacers come in sets of two, or occasionally four. Never use more than one spacer per wheel. If you need more spacing, buy thicker spacers instead of doubling up.

The wheel is a little dirty, but you can see the Wilwood brake kit filling the wheel nicely and the red of the caliper peeking through to tell you this is no stock setup.

And in the rear, having the Wilwood kit shows that I went through the whole car, not just the front end. It's a nice finished look that is sure to impress when the car is parked or driving on the track.

UPGRADING TRANSMISSION AND DRIVELINE

Transmissions and drivelines are often overlooked in the pursuit of high performance, but some critical advantages can be obtained with just a couple of thoughtful modifications in this area.

Most E36 models under consideration for performance modifications and upgrades are manual shift cars. The simple reason is that enthusiasts planning a performance build generally have limited their purchase to manual cars. This is smart because a conversion from automatic to manual shift is an unnecessary expense and a large expense when you have so many manual cars to choose from. If you do have an automatic transmission car, it's best to leave it with the automatic and focus on the performance changes that offer a good return on investment.

Before I begin, let's take a step back and note that all E36 models are rear-wheel drive and use a longitudinally mounted engine and transmission, connected via a two-piece driveshaft to a center-mounted differential with independently suspended axle half-shafts. This classic design offers great performance potential and aids in the great handling characteristics of the E36.

The single most cost-effective thing you can do to improve acceleration, especially from a standing start, is to give the car a more advantageous final drive ratio. M3 models came with 3.15, 3.23, and 3.38 ratios, which are all a big improvement over the stock 328i ratio of 2.93.

The stock setup for a manual transmission in an E36 is pretty good, but you can improve shifting on an older car by replacing the bushings and using an aftermarket short shifter. And you can install a better shift knob, too.

Jumping ahead to the end, the best performance upgrade option with the E36 drivetrain is to upgrade to a higher numerical ratio differential. Remember that higher numerical ratios yield "lower" gears. Return on major investment is highest with this upgrade. Also, a short shifter costs almost nothing and delivers a good upgrade relative to its cost.

E36 Transmissions

The transmissions used in any E36 are interchangeable between all E36 models as well as some E46 models. All E36 models were delivered with manual or automatic transmissions. Depending on the year and model, two different Getrag manual units and two different ZF manual units were offered. Three automatics were offered along with one 5-speed and two 4-speed manuals.

All early E36 manual-shift models used the Getrag transmissions through 1995, and the 318 and 323 models continued to use the Getrag boxes through the end of E36 production in 1998. The 1995 M3 used the first ZF transmission, and then, from 1996 to 1998, both the M3 and the 328 used an upgraded ZF unit. The ZF transmissions are generally considered to be more robust than the Getrag units. Both the ZF and Getrag units use about the same gear ratios. The ratios for the ZF transmission are: (first to fifth) 4.2, 2.49, 1.66, 1.24, and 1.00. Getrag ratios differ by only a few hundredths.

E36 automatic transmissions use a conventional torque converter with solenoid-actuated lockup at highway speeds. From 1992 to 1996, all E36 models equipped with an automatic transmission used a 4-speed unit. Starting in 1996 to the end of the model line, the M3 used a 5-speed unit when an automatic transmission was ordered.

The notable thing about E36 automatics is that they incorporate substantially higher gear ratios than the manual transmissions. For example, in the 4-speed automatic, top gear is 0.72:1, as opposed to 1:1 in fifth gear on the manual transmissions. Because of this gearing difference, the final drive ratio in the differentials shipped with automatics is correspondingly lower.

Transmission Replacement and Upgrade Options

Although all-out race cars may benefit from a custom transmission with sequential shift or "dog box" gears, the standard 5-speed ZF manual transmission delivered with 1996–1998 328 and M3 E36 models is a good solid unit that can handle as much power as most owners develop for street and track use.

However, if an upgrade is desired, starting with the 1996 model year, the European-Spec E36 M3 was delivered with a 6-speed Getrag unit that offered a 0.83:1 overdrive top gear. Gears one through five, however, were identical to the U.S.-spec 5-speed unit. This transmission was carried over to the U.S.-spec E46 line in the 330 and M3, so examples are widely available.

The good news is that this 6-speed is a direct replacement that mates to all E36 6-cylinder engines. You need the transmission itself, plus the shift linkage, driveshaft, and an E46 differential (or you can have the driveshaft mating flange changed to match the E46 driveshaft).

The downside of the 6-speed conversion is that it's expensive. The transmission itself costs about $1,200, plus the other parts and labor. For that money, you have only the 0.83:1 overdrive gear. Unless you want more top speed, that's probably not a great investment. However, you can also use a limited-slip differential from an automatic with a shorter final drive ratio to deliver a closer ratio on the five-six upshift. For example, on the 5-speed, you're shifting from 1.23 to 1.00 from fourth to fifth gear, a 0.23 difference. If you use the 6-speed, the last shift is from 1.00 to 0.83 for a 0.17 difference. But that's a lot of expense to save 0.06 on the last shift.

The Getrag 6-speed units are non-serviceable. No internal parts are available for rebuild and the supply is dwindling. Don't count on these units being available for long. The ZF 6-speed sold in the E46 330-ci ZHP is serviceable and is almost identical to the Getrag unit sold in the E46 M3. Look to swap in the ZF unit if at all possible because the ZF is serviceable and reputedly a more robust transmission.

Manual Transmission Shifting

Both the Getrag and the ZF manual transmissions used in the E36 series are solid and reliable units. Only one reason exists for them to fail early: bad driving. The transmission is made of steel and aluminum and it's not indestructible. Smooth shifts rely on a set of synchronizers that gently press against each other to encourage the motion shafts to spin together as you select the gears. As the gears come together and you release the clutch, torsional and shear forces are applied to the various bearings, gear teeth, and axle joints throughout the drivetrain.

If you stop and think about it, being rough with the gears makes no sense at all. Abusing the gearbox does not help you go faster. Slamming a car into gear at full throttle at the moment the clutch is engaging makes the car jump, upsetting traction as well as applying a hammer blow throughout the engine, drivetrain, and suspension. Once, I watched in horror as a guy destroyed the transmission in his brand-new Audi during the course of a single 30-minute open track practice session. He did it by hammering each shift until the third and fourth gear synchros just gave up and died.

Conversely, the best racing drivers in the world are silky smooth with their shifts. They hold the shift lever lightly in their hands, and they touch it only when selecting a gear. Their shifts are not slow, but not faster than the machinery can handle, either. You can hear race drivers making snap shifts when you watch a race, but remember that those are exotic sequential or dog ring gearboxes, which are built for that kind of treatment, and they are rebuilt after every race.

When you drive, treat the clutch and the shift lever like they're made of thin glass. You can learn to shift the car both quickly and smoothly. If the car jerks or the gears don't want to engage smoothly, back off, slow down, and make sure you're doing it right. You will be rewarded with years of reliable service from the clutch and gearbox.

Many E36 models come with a clutch delay valve. This is a restricted orifice that slows the clutch engagement when releasing the pedal. The delay valve smooths out bad clutch use, but it can be detrimental for performance driving because the clutch engages more slowly and with less precision. Removal is a simple process and well worth the effort if your E36 has one installed.

Short Shifters and Shift Knobs

The stock shift lever is long and includes vibration dampening. The result is that you have to move the shifter farther to select the gears, and the feeling of the shift gates is somewhat numbed. A short shifter helps reduce the time required to make a shift and gives more feedback from the mechanical components.

Tip: Although a short shifter is quicker and more responsive, you also have to make sure your shifting style is impeccable. Don't jam the car into gear or rely on the synchros in the transmission to overcome a great RPM difference. You end up wearing out the synchros unless you learn to treat the short shifter right.

For the touch surface, the stock shift knob BMW gives you is good, but it's an item that many folks like to replace. Carbon fiber and wooden knobs are popular and stylish, but for true high-performance applications, you can't beat a leather-covered knob for positive grip.

If you select an aftermarket knob, make sure it has the right threads or seal to attach to your shift lever and that the threaded part of the knob is well attached. You wouldn't want the knob to come off in your hand! To remove the stock shift knob, just give it a good pull. It comes right off.

Project: Installing a Short Shifter

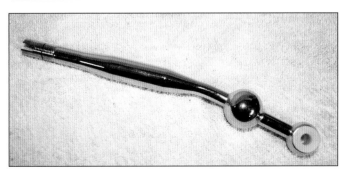

This is the bushing that needed a little drill work to fit the pin used in the 328i. It's soft plastic, so it drilled out nice and easy.

A common aftermarket short shifter from eBay. This one required us to drill out the white bushing a little, but it was otherwise a direct-fit replacement for the stock unit.

You can see that the aftermarket unit is longer from the ball to the bushing. Leverage makes the shift throw shorter at the other end.

Several aftermarket houses make short shifter units for BMW performance enthusiasts. You can also use BMW shifters from certain models to achieve the same effect.

For the E36, the OEM shifter to use is from a Z3 M Roadster, but it might have to be bent to work in the available space. The fact that these M shifters cost about twice the price of an aftermarket shifter leads most people to buy aftermarket.

Even with different designs, all short shifters work on the same principle. You can reduce the throw length between gears by changing the relative lengths of the ends of the shift lever on either side of the ball that acts as a fulcrum. This allows you to shift gears more quickly, but you must first know how to shift your car smoothly, or you damage the transmission over time.

The main distinction between the various shifters is whether they are adjustable or not. Adjustable short shifters allow you to change the lengths on either side of the fulcrum ball by a little bit, which allows you to adjust the shifting throw.

Tip: BMW short shifters are far easier to install if you have disconnected the front end of the driveshaft. If you have the driveshaft disconnected for a clutch job, a short shifter costs $30 to $50, so it's a good time to do it.

This procedure installs a basic solid short shifter in the project 328i.

Follow These Steps

1 Remove the stock shift knob by pulling it off the shift lever. This may not be easy, but it does come off. Then squeeze and remove the shift boot and its mounting ring from the console. Looking down, you can see a foam insert; remove

that too. Underneath that you can see a rubber seal. This pushes down quite easily, but if you can, work the lower lip out and pull it out through the top so it isn't in the way later.

With the shift knob and boot removed, you can see the foam insulation and the lower boot seal on the stock shift lever. The shift knob pulls right off the stock lever, but threads onto the replacement.

You can replace this transmission tunnel to shift lever seal if necessary, but it usually comes out in good enough shape to reuse if you're not too picky about it.

Removing the shift seal, you can see the bushing and the mechanism below. A special tool removes this bushing in minutes, but you can do it with ordinary shop tools with a little finesse.

2 Raise the car up on one side and support it with one or two jack stands. A lift makes this job a lot easier if you have access to one.

3 Slide under the car and reach up around the front end of the driveshaft. You can feel the bottom end of the stock shifter and the shift linkage. A cast-aluminum housing holds the fulcrum ball of the shifter, and the linkage has a round shaft that goes through the loop at the bottom of the shifter. That shaft is held in place by a wedge-shaped circlip that fits into a groove around the round shaft. Two springy arms hold the circlip in place around the shaft. In addition, thin yellow washers reside on either side of the shifter loop, held in place by the circlip and the linkage.

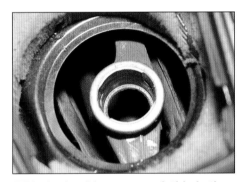

With the bushing removed, this is the shift socket that holds the ball of the shift lever. The actual shift rod is farther down, just above the driveshaft.

4 You can now appreciate the challenge of this project. You must either disconnect the driveshaft to move it out of the way, or work around the driveshaft. It is possible to do this project without removing the driveshaft, but you have to work by feel. Use a long, thin screwdriver (or a small pry-bar with a bend in the shaft) to carefully pry the circlip off. It removes easily. Be careful not to lose it. In this test case, the circlip fell

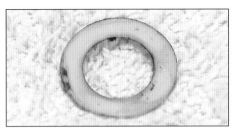

This washer is easy to lose and rides against the pin that goes through the bushing of the shift lever. The spring clip (not shown) is also easy to lose, so be careful.

down between the heat shielding and the transmission tunnel; I had to loosen the heat shielding to find it. The outer yellow washer also fell off and was found on the floor. With the circlip and washer removed, you can pull the shifter and the linkage apart.

5 Now move into the driver's or passenger's seat of the car. With the rubber shift seal removed you can see the top of the fulcrum ball in its plastic cage bushing. The bushing is clipped into the carrier of the shift linkage. If you elect to replace all the shift bushings, this carrier must be removed. This cannot be done without disconnecting the driveshaft, so it's a good task to go along with a clutch replacement.

6 To remove the shifter, you must release the plastic cage bushing that encircles the fulcrum ball. Looking at the bushing from above, you see several segments around the perimeter of the bushing. Two of those segments appear different from the others; they are the two locking tabs. BMW has a special tool to release this bushing, but you can remove it with a pair of small screwdrivers with some patience. Both tabs must be pressed inward to clear indentations in the carrier housing. When the tabs are pressed inward, tap the bushing in a counterclock-

wise direction to clear the indentations. Then pull up on the shifter and the bushing comes out.

Tip: Be sure to compare the size of the loop in the stock shifter with the loop in the replacement shifter. The aftermarket shifter I purchased from eBay had a plastic insert bushing with an interior diameter that was smaller than the stock shifter loop. I measured the stock hole and reamed out the aftermarket plastic bushing on the drill press, and then it fit perfectly.

7 Once liberated from the carrier, the plastic bushing pulls off of the stock shifter easily, and you can press the new shifter into the bushing. Then put the bushing back into the carrier. It snaps into place. The shifter spins freely in the bushing, so make sure that the bend in the shift lever is oriented correctly, toward the rear of the car.

8 Now move back underneath the car. First, make sure the second washer has not fallen off the linkage shaft. Then put the linkage shaft through the loop in the shifter and replace the outer washer. You will have to do this by feel if you have not removed the driveshaft. Finally, replace the circlip; you can press it into place with your fingers. Check to make sure you didn't lose the outer washer and that the circlip is firmly in place. The circlip is still able to spin around in its groove when it is in place.

9 Lower the car to the ground and test the shifting action; if there's any interference with the driveshaft, you need to fix that now. This is typically an issue only with some adjustable units at the extreme limit of their adjustment. Put the car into all five gears and reverse to test for interference.

10 Replace the rubber shift seal, and work the lower lip under the sheet metal. Then replace the foam insert pad and the leather shift boot. Finally, you can press or thread on the shift knob.

The new short shift lever is installed, along with a fresh cage bushing and a billiard ball shift knob. The result is a quick and crisp shifting action that befits a performance car.

I bought the most inexpensive shifter I could find (on eBay), and when I drilled the loop to fit the linkage shaft, installation was easy! The results are spectacular. Instead of a long passenger-car throw, the BMW now shifts like a direct-shift car like a Miata or MGB. For such a small part, a short shifter offers a great improvement in your driving experience.

E36 Clutch Basics

E36 manual transmissions use a single-disc clutch with a dual-mass flywheel, which simply means that the flywheel is an assembly of plates and springs designed to smooth out the torque pulses from the engine and deliver smooth engagement. If your E36 has accumulated more than about 100,000 miles since new, you should have the flywheel inspected and likely replaced if you are performing a clutch upgrade.

Tip: Most stock dual-mass flywheels are worn out completely at 100,000 miles. A thunking sound on driveline engagement or disengagement identifies this failure.

The stock clutch in the E36, whether the transmission is Getrag or ZF, is a strong unit, and should not need to be replaced as a matter of course when you increase engine power. If you make major changes such as installing an S65 V-8 or a turbocharger or supercharger kit, you might need to upgrade the clutch. If so, several aftermarket high-performance clutches are available. Absent a high-power engine, however, there is really no performance benefit to a clutch upgrade.

However, generally speaking, when replacing a clutch disc, be sure to replace the pressure plate, throwout bearing, pilot bearing, plastic pivot pin, clutch fork, shift

rod seal, crankshaft rear main seal, and possibly the transmission input shaft seal at the same time. Those parts may not all be worn enough to require replacement, but the process of accessing the clutch is generally difficult and expensive, so replacing all components with new is a good idea.

Final Drive and Differential

The best speed secrets are those that are easy to improve, and one of the best is the final drive gear. Just like riding a bicycle up a hill, choosing the right gears makes the difference between power pedaling and bogging down.

The stock flywheel is a dual-mass device with internal springs for smooth uptake. For a performance build, you want to replace this with a lighter single-mass flywheel. Most of the expense of a clutch job is in the labor, so don't skimp on this.

On an E36, the stock clutch disc is not sprung, so if you upgrade the flywheel, be sure to buy the whole aftermarket clutch kit with a sprung disc.

The pressure plate is pretty standard; a new one comes with the aftermarket clutch kit, designed for use in a high-performance situation.

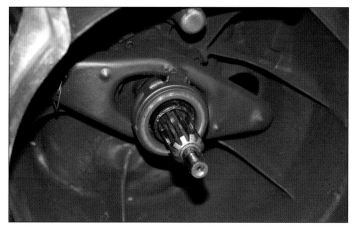

Here's the part some people neglect and live to regret. The throwout bearing should be replaced any time you're working on the clutch. It's a cheap part that is annoying or debilitating if it fails. They tend to fail right after you put in a new high-force clutch, so make sure you replace it.

Stock Final Drive Ratios for E36

The table below shows you the stock final drive ratios delivered with each model in the E36 line. The 318 uses a smaller, less robust unit that is not transferable to 6-cylinder E36 models.

Model	Ratio	Model	Ratio
318 Manual	3.45	328, 323 Automatic	3.91
318 Automatic	4.44	M3 1995 Manual	3.15 Limited-slip
325 Manual	3.15	M3 1996–1998 Manual	3.23 Limited-slip
325 Automatic	3.91	M3 5-Speed Automatic	3.38 Limited-slip
328, 323 Manual	2.93		

Which Final Drive Ratio Do I Have?

You can find the gear ratio and limited-slip status of any E36 differential by looking at the metal tab attached to the back of the final drive assembly. Limited-slip differentials have a stamped number that begins with "S" followed by the ratio, while open differentials begin with the ratio.

You can read this tag on any E36 diff and final drive assembly to see what you have. The first three numbers are all that matters; this indicates a 2.93 ratio. If it was a limited-slip, it would begin with S.

This new differential has a tag that says "S391," indicating a 3.91 ratio and the "S" for limited slip. A freshly rebuilt limited-slip is tighter and more effective than one out of a high-mileage car, and BMW limited-slip devices can be rebuilt to the specifications for tighter control.

As with every performance decision, choosing gears involves tradeoffs. Lower ratio "tall" gears give you faster speed at a given RPM, while "short" gears sacrifice top speed to improve acceleration off the line. The correct gearing for best performance depends on the engine's torque and horsepower, and what you want to do with the car. Torque helps the engine pull the car "out of the hole" at low speeds, while horsepower helps the car maintain top speed at high engine revs.

Autocrossers typically want the shortest gears they can find to maximize acceleration between corners. Land-speed record seekers go to the opposite extreme. They want the tallest gears they can find to maximize top speed. Most of the rest of us like something in the middle that makes sense for the kind of driving we do. If you plan on long highway trips, you want a taller final drive than someone who wants to maximize 0–60 acceleration and doesn't mind turning 3,500 rpm to cruise on the freeway.

Tip: You can make minor changes to the final drive ratio by fitting smaller or larger wheels and tires to your car. Online calculators can help you determine the effect on drive ratio of changing overall tire diameter.

The easiest place to set up custom gearing in any car is in the final drive. In an E36, you have one convenient and easy-to-replace unit (often called a "pumpkin") at the back of the car.

Effects of Changing the Final Drive Ratio

As mentioned, changing the final drive ratio trades off acceleration for top speed. Because most performance cars don't run at top speed very often or for very long, chang-ing to a shorter final drive is usually advantageous with very little downside. This is the least expensive way to have truly breathtaking acceleration with a 323, 325, or 328.

If you have one of the many 323, 325, or 328 models with 2.93 or 3.15 gears, you can benefit from swapping to a 3.23, or 3.38 limited-slip from an M3, or to a 3.91 from an automatic transmission car. All 6-cylinder E36 differentials are a direct swap. Things get a little more complicated when installing the differential from an E46; it involves the axle half-shaft flanges as well as the differential unit itself.

A quick and easy way of estimating the difference in speed-at-RPM in any gear is simply to look at the difference between the ratio numbers. Without getting into too much math, divide the new ratio by the old ratio. For example, if you are considering a change from 2.93 to 3.23: $3.23 \div 2.93 = 1.10$.

So, the RPM the engine must turn to drive at 70 mph on the freeway is multiplied by 1.1. Let's say it's 2,600 rpm in fifth gear with the 2.93 final drive. The new engine speed for the same 70 mph is about 3,000 rpm.

Here's the math if you change to a 3.91 final drive: $3.91 \div 2.93 = 1.33$.

With this final drive, the 70 mph at 2,600 rpm becomes about 3,500 rpm, a much more significant change.

Tip: diffsonline.com has an excellent downloadable Excel spreadsheet in its Technical Information section that does the math for you. The spreadsheet uses the actual tire size and the final drive and gear ratios to give precise answers. You can also buy custom E36 differential units from this company; it features a wide variety of final drive ratios and limited-slip devices.

One great thing about the E36 design is that the speedometer reading is taken from the final drive itself, so the speedometer is still accurate after the change. Note, however, that the BMW speedometer reading from the final drive assumes you are using the standard size tires, so if you have changed tire size, the speedometer may be off.

Limited-Slip Devices

The final drive gears also include the car's differential. Differentials are the devices that allow the wheels to turn at slightly different speeds during cornering for smooth driving. However, a completely open differential allows a drive wheel to spin freely if it lacks traction, and no power goes to the drive wheel that still has traction. That's why performance cars universally use limited-slip differentials; with these units, wheelspin is limited mechanically and distributed between both drive wheels on the E36.

The stock limited-slip differentials delivered with E36 models use a traditional friction clutch system to reduce slip. Essentially, when one axle begins turning faster than the other (for example, the outside wheel during cornering), pressure builds to compress a clutch disc, encouraging the other side to turn at the same speed. This is generally known as "lockup" and is expressed as a percentage. A 25-percent lockup is looser than 50 percent. Over time, the clutch discs wear, reducing lockup, and should be replaced. When rebuilding a limited-slip differential, you can increase lockup to make the system "tighter" by using more clutch discs, or you can change to a different mechanical system (such as a Quaife or OS Giken) altogether.

For most street and track purposes, the friction disc system works very well with fresh components.

A used limited-slip differential can be purchased online for a few hundred dollars, but it is generally best to assume that any such differential needs to be freshened. A professional gear shop should do this work, because clearances must be reset to avoid unusual wear. You can also buy freshly rebuilt differentials set to your preferred final drive ratio and with your preferred lockup or alternative limited-slip device installed. These differentials can range up to several thousand dollars.

The 1996 and later E36 models may be equipped with ASC+T (Automatic Stability Control + Traction, labeled ASC on the console). The ASC+T system is designed to limit wheelspin by applying brake pressure to a free-spinning drive wheel. In addition, the system maintains stability by modulating the engine and applying brake pressure to any wheel as necessary to prevent loss of control. Obviously, this system may interact with a retrofitted limited-slip differential, but M3 models were shipped with both ASC+T and limited-slip differentials.

Project: Installing a Limited-Slip Differential

This procedure installs a replacement differential and final drive unit in the project 1996 328i. I found a freshly rebuilt 4.10 final drive with standard 2-disc limited-slip device and new bearings and seals. This upgrade took the 328 from a basic street car to a vehicle with impressive acceleration. Coming out of corners, the tight limited-slip really helps the car lay down power, and it's easy to stay in the power band. With the car's stock 6,300 rpm redline, top speed is still right around 118 mph in fifth gear. Cruising at 70 mph on the freeway happens at 3,750 rpm.

This project involves dropping the exhaust and disconnecting the axle half-shafts and the driveshaft. If you are planning to install rear subframe chassis reinforcements, adjustable rear camber arms, or a cat-back exhaust, this is a great time to double up those projects because you have to disassemble the same area to perform those installations.

The time required for this project is about an hour. M8 or M10 Torx bolts hold the drive axles to the final drive flange so you will need a special tool to remove them.

Follow These Steps

1 Put the car on a lift or securely rest it on a set of quality jack stands. You can see the rear axles and the final drive unit bolted into its cradle. It's easiest if the car is in neutral so the driveshaft turns freely.

2 Disconnect and remove the rear sway bar; you can leave the drop links in place. Also remove the cat-back portion of the exhaust system.

You have to disconnect the sway bar and remove the cat-back exhaust before you can access the differential cage in the rear subframe.

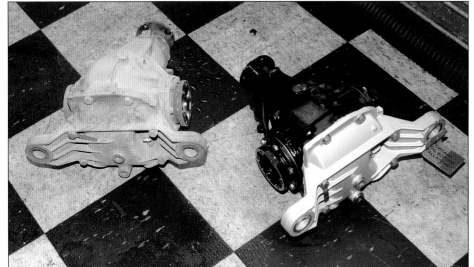

The old differential is on the left, and the new limited-slip differential is on the right. This upgrade is about to change the project 328i from zero to hero.

3 Disconnect the four driveshaft bolts and disconnect the driveshaft. You need to use combination wrenches here, as there is no room for a socket. There is a little fore-and-aft motion available because of the two-piece design of the driveshaft. BMW recommends using new nuts with these bolts when you reassemble.

The driveshaft disconnects with just four bolts. There's enough play at the splined yokes that you can move it forward to disengage the bolts.

The mating flange of the differential shows the positions of the four driveshaft bolts. Those bolts take up all of the shear forces of the engine's torque every time the car moves.

4 Disconnect the axle half-shafts from the final drive flanges. These use male Torx head bolts, so you need a set of Torx sockets to loosen them. Air tools might come in handy here, especially if the axles have not been removed because they were installed at the factory. Once disconnected, you can hold the axles out of the way with safety wire or let them rest on the subframe.

Undo the Torx bolts that hold the axle half-shafts to the differential axle flanges. These may be very hard to undo, so be careful and take your time.

The axle flange on each side of the differential shows where the six Torx bolts thread in.

You can see that the axle has a bulge that fits into the recess on the differential axle flange. This helps keep everything in place and deal with torque shear.

5 Disconnect the wiring plug for the speedometer sensor and fold the wire out of the way.

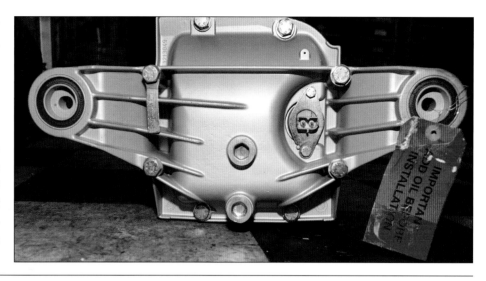

This is the part of the differential you see most often. At the bottom is the oil drain plug. In the middle is the oil fill plug. The speedometer plugs in at the middle-right. And the new bushings are out on the wings. The tab indicating the ratio is at middle-left.

6 Support the final drive unit with a jack. The unit weighs about 75 to 80 pounds, and you don't want it falling on your head! Then, undo the three bolts that hold the final drive unit to the rear subframe. Two are on the rear and one is on the front of the final drive unit.

The differential assembly weighs about 80 pounds, so support it when you're getting ready to remove it. You don't want this falling on your foot.

7 Gently slide the final drive unit rearward and tip it out of the rear subframe carrier.

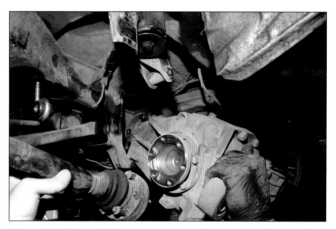

The old differential comes out to the rear and must be angled down to clear the rear subframe cage in which it rides.

Keep the differential supported as you remove it from the cage. It comes out easily but requires some muscle to move it around.

8 Fill the new final drive unit with good quality synthetic gear oil, or check that it is adequately filled.

Before you fill, remove the oil drain plug to be sure there is no oil in the differential already. As a new rebuild, this one was dry. So I carefully re-torqued the drain plug and got ready to fill the differential.

I use Royal Purple gear oil in my differentials. Synthetic oil is the way to go because the limited-slip device generates some heat. This oil also keeps the bearings in good shape for the life of the car.

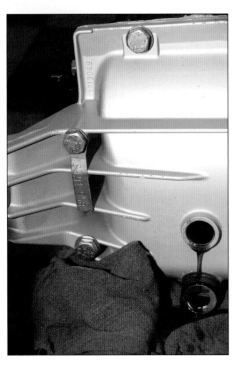

With the differential out of the car, you can use a short length of fuel hose to make filling the differential with oil an easy task.

You know the differential is full to the correct level when the oil flows back out the filling port. Make sure the differential is level for the correct amount.

9 If you are planning to replace the bushing in the final drive carrier, you must remove the subframe and press out the old bushing and press the new one into place.

This bushing should be replaced, but you need to have the whole rear subframe out to do it. I will come back to this and replace it when I reinforce the subframe mounts and install the lower rear camber control arms.

10 Installation generally goes in reverse order of steps 1–7, but place all of the fasteners on loosely before you tighten any of them. Be sure to check torque specs in the factory shop manual and set torques on all fasteners with a quality torque wrench.

When it's all back together, test drive the car gently and listen for any unusual sounds coming from the driveshaft, final drive, and drive axles. If you installed a limited-slip differential, try some sharp turns at low speed and you should be able to feel it working.

Here's the new differential in place and connected up. You can really tell the limited-slip is working when you're tight-turning at low speeds, and when you can lay down the power anywhere in a corner.

IMPROVING DRIVER COMFORT, SAFETY AND AERODYNAMICS

One of the most important factors in a performance car build is to keep the driver comfortable and safe in the car. You simply cannot drive well if the seat is hurting you or fatiguing you, or if you cannot reach the steering wheel or controls effectively.

Also, as you modify the car for performance you don't want to cut corners in the safety gear. If you move out of street performance and into racing, many of these decisions are written into the preparation rules. You must have a certified racing seat, racing harness, fire extinguisher, and so on, or you won't be racing.

In all the modifications you make, ask yourself if what you're doing will compromise the basic safety margins built into the car from the factory. If it's going to put you in danger to make a mod, reconsider whether you really want to take that risk.

Apart from the expensive gear you put into a performance car, consider carrying a fire extinguisher and a good first aid and winter weather kit. It never hurts to be ready to help others or yourself in an emergency.

Sport or Racing Seats

The car's seats are a vital safety component. Together with the seat belts, air bags, and the body construction, the seats help keep you safe in an accident. Some aftermarket seats are very good, and some are not as good as the stock seats in a crash. Look for an FIA rating on a motorsports seat; it indicates that it has passed stress testing.

But perhaps the biggest area where people compromise the safety of their seats is in the mounting. For street cars, I like to adjust the seat for different drivers; for a race car, people usually bolt the seat right to a welded-in brace for a fixed position. Many aftermarket seat-mounting kits are available, and you should look carefully at any kit and choose one that is solid and well made. Because the seats are so critical to your safety, you should have any aftermarket seats installed by a professional.

Grab the back of a seat and shake it back and forth. The stock seat moves some, and an old and worn seat may move quite a bit. An after-

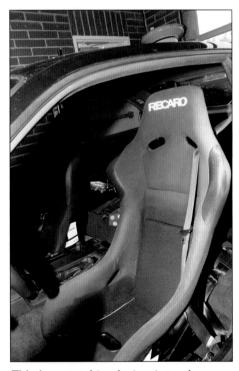

This is a good try, but not good enough. This owner has disconnected the safety belt and run it through the holes in a racing seat, but where will he buckle the belt? If it passes through the other hole, will he be able to fasten the belt low and tight across his hips? If not, this implementation will not help him in a crash. He should invest in racing belts to use this seat.

A racing seat has certain design characteristics to enhance driver performance and safety. Note the big side and hip bolsters to keep you in place. Also note the holes to accommodate the shoulder and lap belts. Do not use the stock three-point harness with a racing seat. It's not safe.

If more than one person drives your track car, use an adjustable mount. This allows you to slide the seat forward and aft while maintaining the benefits of a racing seat.

For a street car, a good sport seat should offer improved side bolstering to hold the driver in place and good lumbar support, but it should not impede the stock three-point seat belt system.

market performance seat, properly installed, should move very little. A hard-mounted FIA-rated racing seat should flex a little, but not move.

One more thing to note about seats is that most FIA-rated racing seats have a fixed position; you can't adjust the angle of the seatback. The hinges and stops that allow you to adjust the rake of the seatback are a weak point and have been known to break or give way in an accident. You can choose adjustable racing seats, but they are not common. Also, because of the high side bolsters and shoulder supports, most racing seats do not work correctly with stock seat belts and require a racing harness to properly hold you in the car.

Safety Belts and Harness Bars

As you increase the performance level, think about increasing your safety gear as well. As mentioned before, a good racing seat helps hold you in place not just in an accident, but also as you drive. The second half of that equation is the driver and passenger harness. A good five- or six-point racing harness, well-attached, keeps you planted in the seat, so you're not expending energy or attention on keeping your body under control while you drive. Leading manufacturers of quality harnesses are Simpson, G-Force, Willans, Sabelt, Schroth, and others. Look for a harness that is SFI- or FIA-rated. SFI-rated harnesses are considered "good" for two years while an FIA-rated one is good for

five years. They cost similar amounts so try and find one that has an FIA rating on it.

The four-point "sport" belts on the market are not real racing harnesses and suffer from a tendency to ride up on your midsection if you tighten the shoulder belts. In an accident, you want both the lap belts low across your hips and the shoulder belts tight. You need a five- or six-point harness for that, and a proper racing harness costs no more than a four-point, although you will need a seat that accommodates the anti-submarine (ASM) strap between your legs. Schroth makes an ASM–technology belt that has a loop in the right harness designed to break on impact, creating stock-like belt behavior when in an accident. This is the only four-point belt I recommend.

A proper racing harness is not generally recommended for a street car, but it is essential in a dedicated track or racing car. It takes a bit longer to buckle a five-or six-point harness, but it's worth the effort on track. Nothing holds your body in the seat like a racing harness.

Even if you do decide to put a five-point racing harness in your street car, chances are still good that you do not want to weld in a full roll bar with an integrated harness bar. For a racing harness to work properly, it must be installed to a lateral bar running behind the driver's shoulders. Therefore, aftermarket manufacturers have created bolt-in harness bars.

This roll structure includes a lateral harness bar behind the seat. The harness bar has to be set at the right height to create the correct angles for the shoulder belts to be most effective. When you have a roll structure made, bring along your seat and be prepared for a custom fitting.

These provide mounting locations at the correct height and distance for a racing harness. You bolt these bars to the floor of the car behind the driver's and passenger's seats. They make the back seats pretty much useless, so consider a rear seat delete if you plan to install harness bars. Follow the instructions on both the harness bar and on the harness carefully.

Make sure to check carefully that the bar you have selected is not a "harness guide bar." One type of bar is designed to mount the harness shoulder straps to "a harness bar" and another type is designed to simply change the angle of the belts so that they fall within the 22-degree variance that is recommended for shoulder belt angles. This harness "guide" bar is not structurally sound

and cannot have the harnesses mounted to it.

Roll Cages

A good roll cage is a necessity for a car that you plan to drive on a race-track more than a couple of times a year, and if you plan on driving to the limit of the car's potential. In addition to holding the driver's compartment open in a rollover, a roll cage helps stiffen the chassis.

Your choices with roll cages are essentially unlimited because a custom cage can include anything you want. You can also buy a premade "bolt-in" cage kit and install it yourself. Of the two, custom work costs a lot more, but it's worth it. A custom cage is generally (but not always) welded into the chassis of a car. It fits your car better and you can have the builder make the cage as complete or as unobtrusive as you like. A custom cage can also tie into the strut towers and potentially extend from bumper to bumper. Be sure you choose a good cage builder. Someone with experience in the local motorsports business is best, especially if you're building to a set of rules.

Bear in mind that if you choose a bolt-in cage, you'll be drilling some holes through the floorpan and various panels. If you choose a custom cage, you'll be welding plates and potentially penetrating bulkheads in the car. You can remove a bolt-in cage and fill the holes and walk that modification back, but a weld-in cage is forever and limits the resale market of your car to other racing enthusiasts.

Most bolt-in cages are either unsafe or do not have adequate support on the main attachment points to the chassis, so I do not recom-

This is an example of a bolt-in roll cage for very basic use. The reverse bends to clear the dashboard limit this structure's rollover protection; no crossbars or door bars are present to add rigidity and protection there. Not all roll structures are created equal, so pay attention and buy a good one.

Now this is a proper roll cage. The extensive cross-bracing makes this chassis extra rigid and provides great protection for the driver. A car with a good custom cage can take a rollover and still be fixable.

A gusset makes a strong triangle out of a weak connection point. Gussets are one of the big things to look for in a roll structure. This triangle to the right of the steering wheel helps brace the entire structure.

mend them. In some cases bolt-in cages have punched through a car's floor during a rollover.

Gauges and Indicators

Moving to the car's interior, one of the first areas you may want to consider for improvement is the selection of gauges and indicators. In stock form, the E36 offers you comparatively little information.

Most performance enthusiasts want the additional information that extra gauges can provide, plus there's the fact that a bunch of gauges looks pretty cool. You can upgrade as little or as much as you like in this area. Gauges and senders exist to tell you oil temperature and pressure, turbo or supercharger boost (if your car is so equipped), air-fuel mixture, or exhaust gas temperature. Many of

A gauge pod like this one from ATI snaps in place on the stock steering column and holds two standard size small gauges. You can also adjust the angle of each gauge. This is a clean and finished-looking way to add gauges.

A more traditional approach is to make a gauge holder out some sheet metal. This was red-coated sheet aluminum. Some work with tin snips gave us the shape, and I used a bench vise as a bending brake. A 2.25-inch hole saw completed the small gauge installation and it looks great.

Another way to add gauges is to install a pod that mounts on the A-pillar. This looks great, but might be in the way as you enter and exit the driver's seat.

A shift light is another great addition. These are wired into the tachometer or take a signal from the OBD-II port and light up when the engine reaches a preset RPM. You don't have to take your eyes off the road when it's time to shift.

these gauges plug directly into the vehicle's existing OBD-II port and so do not require any difficult wiring work. They are simply reading information that the BMW's DME system is already recording.

However, the factory DME readings are not always very accurate or responsive, because many of them are there for monitoring purposes only. The best and most accurate way to get information from the car is still to tap directly into whatever system you want to read with an independent sender unit instead of relying on the factory DME readings.

You can buy gauge pods (some made of fancy carbon fiber) that fit on the dashboard or steering column. These typically allow you to install up to four gauges of a standard size.

Hooking up aftermarket gauges can be tricky because many sensor locations are inconvenient and require special tools to access. Also, in general, critical sensors such as exhaust gas temperature should be calibrated to the gauge being used. Consult an experienced shop for help with gauge selection and installation.

Aftermarket Steering Wheels

The car's steering wheel is another safety component, because it houses the driver's air bag. Aftermarket steering wheels look and feel great, but you don't generally keep the car's airbag. It can also be difficult to make the horn and the automatic turn signal cancelers work with an aftermarket wheel.

Among manufacturers of steering wheels, Momo is the leader in import fitments. Grant also makes a variety of aftermarket wheels, and some are much less appropriate than others for performance applications. In any case, the main advantage of an aftermarket wheel is in the ability to custom-select the diameter and configuration of the wheel and the thickness of the outer ring. Select a wheel that is comfortable for you to hold. Remember that a larger diameter wheel gives you more steering leverage, and even with power steering you may find turning a small wheel to be more of a chore than you expected.

You can also buy a quick-release kit for the wheel. Many racers use

MOMO makes great sport steering wheels. They're usually leather-wrapped and MOMO adapters are available for virtually any car on the market from any era.

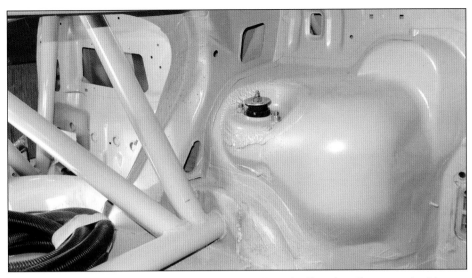

Here's how a roll cage reinforces the car's chassis. By tying the rear strut tower into the cage, you're taking a point that is subject to a lot of force and making it a rigid part of a big arch that is also tied to the front strut towers.

these because they allow you to bring the wheel closer to you, but you can pop the wheel off the steering column for easy entry and exit from the driver's seat.

Note that E36 or E46 aftermarket steering wheels require removal of the wheel's clockspring for installation. Unless something new has arrived on the market recently it is a certainty that you will lose the turn signal canceling, horn, and air bag with an aftermarket wheel.

Sound-Deadening Materials

Some people enjoy the sound of their car's engine and the rumble of the road, but others want a quiet ride. If you're a fanatic for quiet, you can improve on the stock sound deadening. Products such as Dynamat or Second Skin really cut down on road and engine noise in the cabin.

For an easy project, you can pull the console and other trim pieces and then insert the padding behind them, as shown. If your goal is much more quiet, you can pull the entire interior and line the entire cabin with sound deadening pads.

Chassis Braces and Reinforcements

All E36 models use a unibody design, which is to say, the chassis and body are made of stamped pieces of sheet steel welded together. In hard cornering, the chassis is subjected to a great deal of pressure, and it flexes. Chassis flex works against the suspension, slightly changing its geometry at the worst possible time.

Ideally, you want the chassis to be as stiff as possible. The main points of flex are at the strut towers and suspension subframes, where the forces from the suspension are concentrated. Strut tower bars bridge the strut towers across the top of the engine bay, making an arch that helps stiffen the chassis. At the front and rear subframes, the E36 has a tendency to rip the mounting points out of its unibody pan; weld-in kits reinforce those points. For ultimate chassis stiffening, however, you can't beat a good roll cage, and I discuss a few of those as well.

Weld-On Chassis Reinforcements

E36 cars have a confirmed habit of cracking and even ripping out the mounts for the front and rear subframes that carry the suspension. The fix for this is easy enough: You need to weld in supporting material around the subframe pickup points. These are essentially big washers that take the strain otherwise placed on the unibody mounting points. This upgrade is an absolute necessity for cars with upgraded suspensions and those used on the track.

The rear upper strut mounts have also been known to rip out of the chassis. A stock Z3 part can be purchased from BMW for about $10, and this part adds a small plate to the top of the rear strut mount and helps distribute the load. Similar parts are available in the aftermarket.

Because the fix requires removal of the subframes, this kind of project is very well suited to be performed at the same time as a final drive upgrade, suspension upgrade, rear lateral control arm replacement, or rear trailing arm bushing upgrade.

Project: Installing a Front Strut Tower Brace

A front strut tower brace is primarily a dress-up item for most street cars, but over time, it helps the E36 chassis stay strong. The example bar in this project is the polished aluminum bar from H&R. This project was performed on the project 328i, but it works for all E36s.

If you don't have a roll cage to tie everything together, you can start by using strut tower bars. These are easily removed to allow access to the engine for work.

Follow These Steps

1 With the car standing on its wheels normally, undo the six 13-mm nuts that hold the strut tops in position. Place the ends of the strut bar onto the strut top studs and loosely thread the nuts back on, but do not tighten them yet. The ends of the strut bar fit in only one orientation.

2 Each strut tower end has a through-bolt to hold the central part of the bar to the end plates. The central bar is adjustable. Loosely mount one end and adjust the other until it fits between the strut towers.

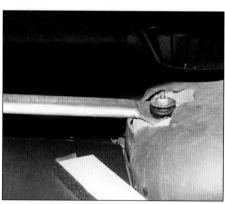

A rear strut bar also works to keep the whole chassis rigid. The forces exerted on the car's chassis through the suspension are enough to twist the unibody significantly.

3 Tighten the strut top mounting nuts, then the passenger-side through-bolt. Finally, tighten the driver-side through-bolt. The hood should shut normally.

Aerodynamic Devices

Quite a few different kinds of aerodynamic devices are in use on cars, and many of them can be installed on an E36. It's helpful to review what they're called and what they're supposed to do. This section briefly reviews the major components in use today.

Wings

Wing is a term generally given to an aerodynamically shaped device that is mounted on braces at the rear of the car, also known as an airfoil. Purpose-built race cars, such as Indy cars, also have wings on the front end of the car, but sedans do not generally use those.

This wing is positioned up in the airflow and has the air foil oriented to create downforce. The panels on the end keep air from spilling off the sides, increasing the air foil's efficiency.

Airfoils work because of their shape: convex on one side and slightly concave on the other. Air flows faster past the convex side than the concave. This creates lower pressure on the convex side, and higher pressure on the concave side, and the

difference in pressure is felt as lift or downforce. The end plates keep air from spilling off the side of the wing, increasing the effect.

A wing on the car is fundamentally the same as a wing on an airplane, but where an airplane uses a

This chin spoiler helps direct air up and through the grille. Brake cooling ducts could go in those other lower holes.

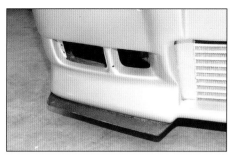

This is an interesting splitter. It helps create a little downforce, and it helps direct air into those intake holes, but that's about it.

wing to generate lift so it can fly, on a car you turn the airfoil upside down to generate downforce, helping stick the car to the ground. For a wing to do you any good, it has to sit in the airflow over the car.

Aftermarket wing makers generally don't have access to the kind of development and testing facilities that the automakers do. Take a look at the wings that professional racers use on their cars if you want to see the result of serious downforce requirements. In addition, budget plays a big part in determining the best possible solution.

Realistically, until you're going well in excess of reasonable street and highway speeds, no wing is going to do a whole lot more than gravity is already doing to pin down the rear end of a 3,500-pound car. So the bottom line is that you should regard a wing as an aesthetic decoration until you're ready for serious racing, and then the wing will likely be specified for you in the racing rules.

Spoilers

Spoilers are often confused with wings because so many spoilers are mounted on the back of a car in the same place as a wing. But if you look closely, a spoiler is not designed to produce downforce.

Rear spoilers improve a car's stability by creating turbulence in the airflow going over the back of the car, negating lift that the car is generating. If you stand back and look at a car from the side, it looks a little like a wing with the roofline as the convex side and the underside as the concave side. Moving that shape through the air can create lift. By disrupting the airflow over the top of the car, you eliminate the wing effect and reduce the amount of lift naturally generated by the shape of the body. Some people also use "chin" or "lip" spoilers on the front of a car to disrupt the air trying to pass underneath the body.

Air Dam

An air dam is a specific kind of spoiler. You see these frequently on track racing cars. They are flexible walls at the front of the car that brush the ground (or come close to it). As the car moves forward, the air dam prevents air from flowing under the car and generates low pressure under the body, sucking the car down to the ground.

Splitters

A splitter is another implementation of the wing idea. With a splitter, you place a flat surface parallel to the ground at the bottom of the front bodywork. By sticking this plane out in front of the car, you create a high-pressure area on top of the plane because the air is running into the car's nose and "piling up." It cannot deflect downward and under the car. With lower pressure air flowing below the splitter, the nose of the car gains some downforce.

Canards

Canard is the French word for a duck. It also means to tell a lie, so how it came to describe little winglets on the front of a car is a mystery. But for our purposes, canards are small airfoils installed in front of the front wheels on the lower fenders. They are designed to add a little bit of downforce, similar to the diving planes on a submarine.

Diffusers

A diffuser is a special kind of spoiler. In this case, it's an anti-spoiler. A diffuser sits underneath the rear bumper area of a car and directs airflow out from beneath the car smoothly into the low-pressure area that the car leaves behind as it moves forward. This helps stabilize the car in the airflow and allows the other aerodynamic devices to work to their best effect, especially splitters and air dams.

PROJECT 328i FINAL BUILD SHEET

The following list shows every part put onto the project 328i in the course of research for this book. You can see how the costs add up quickly! If you plan to build an E36, you should be prepared to incur similar expenses.

Project Specs

1996 BMW 328i	114,000 miles
four-door sedan	no collision damage

Project Modifications & Parts Costs

328i initial purchase	**$3,000**	Whiteline caster bushings	$90
Bentley shop manual	**$60**	OEM tie rods	$125
Engine		OEM bump stops	$100
Injen cold-air intake kit	$129	H&R strut tower bar	$120
Corsa RSC cat-back exhaust	$979	Turner rear camber arms	$200
M50 intake manifold	$100	Turner subframe reinforcements	$260
Turner M50 manifold install kit	$300	Rear trailing arm bushings	$50
S52 M3 camshafts	$200	Turner RTAB limiter kit	$90
Cam chain tensioner	$60	**Brakes**	
Beisan VANOS rebuild kit	$80	Wilwood complete big brake kit	$3,200
Idler and tensioner pulleys	$80	M3 spindles	$400
Valvecover gasket	$30	**Wheels/Tires**	
Fuel injector O-rings	$6	E46 328i 17-inch wheels (street)	$320
Driveline		E36 M3 17-inch wheels (track)	$100
Short shifter	$35	Falken Azenis tires (track)	$440
4.1 limited-slip final drive	$500	10-mm hub-centric wheel spacers	$120
Suspension		**Interior**	
H&R Touring Cup suspension kit	$800	ATI 2-gauge pod	$40
Whiteline bushing kit	$50	VDO water temp gauge	$25
H&R front sway bar kit	$250	VDO oil pressure gauge	$25
H&R rear sway bar kit	$250	Billiard ball shift knob	$0
Replacement A-arms	$400	**Total project car investment**	**$13,014**

Project Analysis

When I started this project, this 328i was tired but still had good engine power and torque. By the end of the project, I had freshened and improved the car in almost every system, at a cost somewhat higher than the current initial purchase price of an M3 in similar condition. Yet that hypothetical M3 might need many of the same tasks performed, so the costs might be comparable.

In the engine, I saw a gain of 30 wheel horsepower, from 170 in stock form to 200 with commonly available modifications. This puts the project 328i at the low end of M3 performance. Of the modifications, the M50 intake manifold was definitely the most effective at raising horsepower, but nothing I did altered torque by more than a few foot-pounds, and not always with a positive result. The stock E36 pink-top fuel injectors and stock fuel pump were more than adequate; the final testing with all engine modifications in place still showed optimal fuel-air mixture throughout the operating band of the engine.

To take this project further, I would certainly consider an exhaust manifold and a catalyst-delete mid-pipe for a track-only build, or a high-flow catalyst mid-pipe for a street-driven car. I would also invest in custom DME tuning, and with these modifications, the project 328i would likely gain horsepower and torque to put it solidly into the E36 M3 performance range.

My opinion is that the cold-air intake, cat-back exhaust, and M50 intake were worth the cost of the projects, but that the S52 cams were not a good value for the limited improvement they provided. They cost horsepower and torque everywhere except above 5,500 rpm. A complete S52 engine swap would cost more money but likely prove to be a better value in the long run, provided the engine was in good condition.

In the drivetrain, the short shifter was a low-cost installation that yielded a good result, and the single largest perceived performance enhancement was the selection of the shorter limited-slip final drive unit. For street driving, the 4.1-ratio final drive is a little short; first gear is required only when starting against an incline. A 3.23 or 3.38 limited-slip final drive from an M3 would be a better choice for a street-driven car.

The H&R suspension and sway bars, Turner and Whiteline bushings, and the new stock replacement parts were all uniformly easy to install and yielded great results. The car's suspension is firm and predictable for track use, yet supple and comfortable for everyday driving. I rate all these modifications as money well spent.

The Wilwood big brake upgrade is similarly impressive. After I obtained the M3 spindles, the kit installed without any more effort than a brake freshening with stock parts, and provides much-improved brake sensation and stopping power. You need to source M3 parking brake parts as well to complete the changeover. Note also that I needed 10-mm hub-centric spacers to allow the stock E36 17-inch M3 wheels to clear the Wilwood components; the E46 17-inch wheels cleared the brakes with no trouble at all.

SOURCE GUIDE

Active Autowerke
9940 SW 168 Ter.
Miami, FL 33157
305-233-9300
store.activeautowerke.com

AR Auto Service
16088A Boones Ferry Rd.
Lake Oswego, OR 97035
503-697-3311
arauto.com

Auto Tech Interiors
949-923-8211
autotechinteriors.com

Bavarian Autosport
275 Constitution Ave.
Portsmouth, NH 03801
800-535-2002
bavauto.com

Beisan Systems
2109 Longwood Dr.
Raleigh, NC 27612
919-676-1939
beisansystems.com

Bilstein of America
14102 Stowe Dr.
Poway, CA 92064
858-386-5900
bilsteinus.com

BimmerWorld
4085 Pepperell Way
Dublin, VA 24084
540-674-3991
bimmerworld.com

BMP Design Inc.
3208 Park Center Dr.
Tyler, TX 75701
800-648-7278
bmpdesign.com

Corsa Performance
140 Blaze Industrial Pkwy.
Berea, OH 44017
440-891-0999
corsaperformance.com

Dinan Corporation
865 Jarvis Dr.
Morgan Hill, CA 95037
800-341-5480
dinancars.com

Eurosport
5200 E Hunter Ave.
Anaheim, CA 92807
800-783-3876
eurosportacc.com

Falken Tire
8656 Haven Ave.
Rancho Cucamonga, CA 91730
800-723-2553
falkentire.com

H&R Springs
3815 Bakerview Spur, #7
Bellingham, WA 98226
360-827-8881
hrsprings.com

Injen Air Intakes
244 Pioneer Pl.
Pomona, CA 91768
909-839-0706
injen.com

Modern Classics
17725 SW Pacific Hwy.
Tualatin, OR 97062
503-783-6444
modernclassicsauto.com

Öhlins USA
703 South Grove St., Ste. C
Hendersonville, NC 28792
800-336-9029
ohlinsusa.com

Red Ranger Whiteline
8580 Milliken Ave.
Rancho Cucamonga, CA 91730
909-476-2860
redranger.com.au

Turner Motorsport
16 South Hunt Rd.
Amesbury, MA 01913
800-280-6966
turnermotorsport.com

Wilwood Engineering
4700 Calle Bolero
Camarillo, CA 93012
805-388-1188
wilwood.com